US NAVY CARRIER AIRCRAFT
VS
IJN YAMATO CLASS BATTLESHIP
Pacific Theater 1944–45

MARK STILLE

First published in Great Britain in 2015 by Osprey Publishing
PO Box 883, Oxford, OX1 9PL, UK
PO Box 3985, New York, NY 10185-3985, USA
E-mail: info@ospreypublishing.com

A CIP catalog record for this book is available from the British Library

ISBN: 978 1 4728 0849 3
PDF ISBN: 978 1 4728 0850 9
ePub ISBN: 978 1 4728 0851 6

Edited by Tony Holmes
All artwork by Jim Laurier
Maps by JB Illustrations
Index by Rob Munro
Typeset in ITC Conduit and Adobe Garamond

Originated by PDQ Media, Bungay, UK
Printed in China through Worldprint Ltd

15 16 17 18 19   10 9 8 7 6 5 4 3 2 1

TBM Avenger versus *Yamato* cover art

The US Navy's second major encounter with a Yamato-class battleship
occurred on April 7, 1945. In an operation without any logic, the IJN sent its
prestige battleship *Yamato* and a small group of escorts against the American
invasion force off Okinawa. The mission had no prospects of success since the
US Navy could throw literally hundreds of carrier aircraft at the Japanese
ships. Such overwhelming air power was sufficient to sink even the most
heavily armored warship. This scene shows *Yamato* under attack by a TBM-3
Avenger torpedo-bomber from VT-84, the unit being embarked in the Essex-
class fleet carrier USS *Bunker Hill* (CV-17). The Avenger is just about to drop
its torpedo some 1,500 yards from the battleship. In three attacks during the
day, between nine and 12 torpedoes and seven bombs hit *Yamato*. The ship
sank far short of its planned destination with heavy loss of life, *Yamato*'s
destruction marking the end of the battleship era, as well as the demise of the
IJN as an ocean-going force. (Cover artwork by Jim Laurier)

SB2C Helldiver versus *Musashi* cover art

The US Navy carrier force first encountered the IJN's Yamato-class battleships
in October 1944 at the battle of Leyte Gulf. On the 24th the main Japanese
force, which included the super battleships *Yamato* and *Musashi*, was attacked
for more than five hours by five groups of Avenger torpedo-bombers and
Helldiver dive-bombers. This scene shows *Musashi* under attack by an SB2C-3
Helldiver from VB-18, embarked in USS *Intrepid* (CV-11), during the first
attack on the battleship which commenced at about 1030hrs. The Helldiver is
nearing the bottom of its dive some 1,500ft above *Musashi*. Of the six
Helldivers that attacked the super battleship in the first wave, four scored near
misses without doing any real damage. Indeed, the only damage inflicted on
Musashi during the first attack was by a single torpedo hit amidships on the
starboard side. *Intrepid*'s dive-bombers and torpedo-bombers played a leading
role in the destruction of *Musashi*, participating in three of the five attacks on
the Japanese force. VB-18 paid a high price for success on this day, however,
losing five Helldivers. (Cover artwork by Jim Laurier)

CONTENTS

INTRODUCTION

The battleship was the measuring stick of every major naval power following its introduction in the late 19th century. At the turn of the 20th century, a major innovation occurred in battleship design which was so radical that all future battleships were known as "dreadnoughts" after the first ship built to this new concept. The dreadnought was the most powerful fighting machine in existence thanks to its combination of big guns, significant armored protection, and speed and range, which allowed it to operate all over the world.

The race to build more dreadnoughts was a factor leading to the outbreak of World War I, which saw the world's leading navy, Great Britain's Royal Navy, engage the navy of Imperial Germany in the North Sea. Despite the expectations of most naval commanders and observers that dreadnoughts would wage a series of battles for control of the North Sea, there was only a single clash between them during the war, and another involving the dreadnought's close cousin, the battlecruiser. These engagements were inconclusive. Dreadnoughts proved to be very tough ships to sink, and neither side dared risk them in unfavorable tactical circumstances.

After World War I, the battleship remained the undisputed arbiter of war at sea. Its vulnerability to torpedoes and mines, and to certain types of fire from other dreadnoughts, was addressed by designers, who increased the ship's underwater and horizontal protection.

The naval rivalry between Great Britain and Germany was replaced with a new rivalry between Great Britain and the United States and between the United States and Japan. All three powers were preparing to embark on a large and possibly ruinous dreadnought-building program. Indeed, the United States' program was so massive that it promised to eclipse Japanese naval power and even surpass the Royal Navy. Faced with this prospect, all sides agreed to a series of naval arms reduction treaties, beginning with the Washington Naval Treaty in 1922. These treaties not only controlled the size and armament of battleships, but limited the numbers that each of the five major naval powers could hold.

Against its will, Japan was forced to accede to a position of inferiority in battleships with a ration of three-to-five compared to the United States and Great Britain. This inferiority was in effect until the start of 1937. At the end of the naval treaty era, Japan took a new route to compensate for its battleship inferiority. The path the Japanese chose was to build a class of super battleship that could create a qualitative overmatch against any other existing or planned foreign rival. This was the genesis of the Yamato class.

Meanwhile, as the battleship remained the essential yardstick by which to compare major naval powers, another type of ship was entering the scene. The first aircraft carriers were little noticed since their small floatplanes or aircraft launched from tiny flightdecks possessed little offensive power. Certainly, these fragile machines posed no threat to the battleship. From these beginnings, the Royal Navy, US Navy and Imperial Japanese Navy (IJN) pressed on with carrier development. Indeed, all three navies made use of battleships or battlecruisers scheduled to be scrapped by the Washington Naval Treaty and converted them into carriers. These ships were able to carry enough aircraft to make them significant strike platforms. The aircraft they embarked were constantly being improved in range and, most importantly, their ability to carry a heavy payload. By the late 1930s the aircraft carrier at last possessed the potential to usurp the battleship as the pre-eminent naval platform.

The promise of the aircraft carrier was quickly realized at the start of World War II. British carriers played a key role in the war in the Mediterranean against the Italian *Regia Marina* and helped sink the German battleship *Bismarck*. In December 1941, the power of the aircraft carrier was put on full display when the IJN raided the main base of the US Navy's Pacific Fleet, sinking five battleships and damaging three more. Although they were all trapped in port, it was clear that the battleship could not stand up to massed air attack and hope to survive.

This is the classic photograph of *Yamato* during its sea trials in October 1941. The shot shows the ship's graceful appearance, with its raked bow and stack. (Naval History and Heritage Command, Photo Archives, Naval Subject Collection)

The US Navy quickly applied the lesson of Pearl Harbor. From the earliest point in the war, the carrier became the centerpiece of American naval striking power in the Pacific. The US Navy's prewar carrier force was small, consisting of only seven fleet carriers (just six of these were suitable for operations in the Pacific). It suffered heavy losses in 1942 stemming the Japanese tide and taking the first steps on the road to Tokyo during the second half of the year in the campaign to take and then hold Guadalcanal, in the southern Solomons. The four carriers lost in 1942 were quickly replaced in 1943 with the first of the Essex-class fleet carriers. Loaded with new aircraft replacing prewar US Navy carrier fighters, dive- and torpedo-bombers, these warships were war-winning instruments of power projection.

As the conflict in the Pacific unfolded, the IJN's carrier force atrophied while the Japanese retained their battleships, especially the two units of the Yamato class, for an expected decisive battle with the US Navy. In mid-1944 the American carrier force destroyed its Japanese counterpart. As the US Navy's advance in the second half of 1944 moved closer to Japan, the IJN was forced to commit its last major asset – its heavy surface units led by the Yamato-class super battleships. The clash of the most powerful carriers in the world against the world's largest battleships was inevitable.

USS *Essex* (CV-9) in May 1945, with a large proportion of Carrier Air Group 83 on the flightdeck. The US Navy's practice of storing aircraft on both the hangar deck and the flightdeck (in what was called a deck park) allowed large numbers – principally Hellcats, Avengers and Helldivers, as seen here – to be embarked. These types duly mounted crippling attacks on Japanese surface units in 1944–45. (Real War Photos)

CHRONOLOGY

1934
October — The IJN's Bureau of Naval Construction begins design work on a new class of super battleship.

1935
May 27 — US Navy begins first aerial tests of the Mark 13 air-launched torpedo.

1936
July — IJN given authorization to build super battleships *Yamato* and *Musashi*.

1937
March — Revised design for Yamato-class super battleships ready.
November 4 — *Yamato* laid down.

1938
March 29 — *Musashi* laid down.
Summer — Mark 13 torpedo enters frontline service.
August — US Navy issues specifications for a new carrier scout bomber that would become the SB2C Helldiver.

1939
March 25 — US Navy issues design requirements for a new carrier-capable torpedo-bomber.
May 15 — Orders for 370 SB2C Helldiver dive-bombers placed with Curtiss prior to the aircraft making its first flight.

1940
August 8 — *Yamato* launched.
November 1 — *Musashi* launched.

Grumman's mock-up of the XTBF-1 in original form, without the dorsal fillet ahead of the vertical fin. The first prototype is thought to have flown once or twice without the fillet, which became standard on all subsequent Avengers to enhance stability. (Grumman)

December	US Navy orders 286 TBF Avenger carrier-capable torpedo-bombers from Grumman.	**October 24**	Battle of the Sibuyan Sea sees more than 250 US Navy carrier aircraft attack First Diversion Attack Force and sink *Musashi*.
December 18	First flight of the XSB2C-1 Helldiver prototype.	**October 25**	Battle off Samar, the centermost action of the battle of Leyte Gulf, sees *Yamato* fire its 18.1-inch guns against US Navy ships for the only time.

1941

August 7	First test flight of the prototype XTBF-1 Avenger torpedo-bomber.
December 16	*Yamato* commissioned.

1942

January	First production TBF Avenger delivered to the US Navy.
April	First TBF Avengers enter fleet service.
June	TBF Avenger makes combat debut during Battle of Midway.
June 30	First flight by a production SB2C Helldiver.
August 5	*Musashi* commissioned.
December 15	First SB2C Helldiver delivery to a fleet squadron.

1943

December 25	A single torpedo launched by the submarine USS *Skate* (SS-305) hits *Yamato*, defeating its underwater protection system.

1944

October 18	Japanese *Sho-1* plan is activated in defense of the Philippines and First Diversion Attack Force, including both *Yamato* and *Musashi*, departs Lingga, near Singapore.
October 20	American forces land on Leyte, in the Philippines.
October 22	First Diversion Attack Force departs Brunei after refueling, bound for Leyte.

1945

March 19	*Yamato* attacked in Inland Sea, Japan, by US Navy carrier aircraft from Task Force 58 but is undamaged.
April 5	Decision made to commit *Yamato* to support suicide attacks (Operation *Ten-Go*) against US Navy invasion fleet off Okinawa.
April 6	*Yamato* departs the Inland Sea for Okinawa.
April 7	*Yamato* sunk by three waves of American carrier aircraft (from Task Groups 58.1, 58.3 and 58.4) in the East China Sea.

From late 1943 onwards, the flightdecks of virtually all Pacific Fleet fast carriers looked just like this through to VJ Day. Here, F6Fs (VF-6), TBMs (VT-6) and SB2Cs (VB-6) of Carrier Air Group 6 run their engines up prior to launching from USS *Intrepid* (CV-11) in early 1944. (US Navy)

DESIGN AND DEVELOPMENT

US NAVY CARRIER AIR GROUP

Going into the Pacific War, US Navy fleet carriers embarked four units – one fighter, one scouting, one dive-bomber, and one torpedo-bomber squadron. The scouting and bombing squadrons were equipped with the same aircraft – the Douglas SDB Dauntless – and performed essentially the same role. Indeed, later in the war the scouting and bombing squadrons were combined. The standard squadron size was 18 aircraft. This number of fighters per carrier air group subsequently proved insufficient in the face of the Japanese air threat, and it had been increased by mid-1942.

Early war experience also showed that the real offensive power of a carrier air group was in its dive-bombers, since the torpedo-bomber squadrons were equipped with obsolescent Douglas TBD-1 Devastators armed with the then unreliable Mark 13 air-launched torpedo. This changed in mid-1942 with the arrival of the Grumman TBF Avenger torpedo-bomber, but problems persisted

TBD-1 Devastator BuNo 0325 of VT-6, embarked in USS *Enterprise* (CV-6), performs a practice drop with a Mark 13 torpedo on October 20, 1941. This particular TBD-1 survived the carnage of the Battle of Midway to eventually become the very last Devastator to be stricken, on November 30, 1944, from the US Navy. The aircraft was subsequently scrapped.

USS *Yorktown* (CV-10), in its Measure 33/10A dazzle camouflage scheme that the ship wore for much of 1944, is seen here in Puget Sound, Washington, in early October of that year. Having just completed a two-month overhaul, it was heading south to Naval Air Station (NAS) Alameda, California, to embark its Carrier Air Group 3. By the time CV-10 participated in the action that sank *Yamato* on April 7, 1945, it had Carrier Air Group 9 on board. (US Navy)

with the Mark 13 torpedo until 1944. This meant that US Navy carriers would have had difficulty dealing with IJN battleships, since bombs dropped from the shallow altitudes used in dive-bombing lacked the kinetic power to penetrate heavily armored decks. Such ordnance could damage, but not sink, heavily armored warships. To sink battleships, effective torpedoes were needed.

The arrival of the Essex-class carrier, and its introduction into combat from August 1943, transformed the war in the Pacific. No fewer than 24 Essex-class carriers were completed, and 14 of them saw action during World War II. Each ship weighed more than 36,000 tons when fully loaded, and they could carry 90+ aircraft. These fast fleet carriers were complemented by nine Independence-class light carriers, each weighing 14,700 tons when fully loaded and typically embarking a carrier air group of 33 aircraft (24 fighters and nine torpedo-bombers). All war-built American fleet and light carriers were fitted with effective antiaircraft weapons and modern electronics, and they operated with the support of an extensive logistics train that elevated them from being individual raiding platforms into the key components of a task group able to project power on a sustained basis virtually anywhere in the central Pacific.

The carrier air group of an Essex-class ship evolved throughout the war. Into 1944, it consisted of a 36-aircraft fighter squadron, a 36-aircraft dive-bomber squadron and a torpedo-bomber squadron equipped with 18 aircraft. On July 31, 1944, authorization was given to reduce the dive-bomber squadron from 36 to 24 aircraft and increase the size of the fighter squadron to as many as 54 aircraft. The size of the torpedo-bomber squadron remained unaltered. At the time of the battle of Leyte Gulf, when the US Navy carrier force encountered the IJN's heavy surface units, Essex-class carrier air groups were in the process of this transition.

In December 1944, in the face of a growing kamikaze threat, carrier air group composition was adjusted again to increase air defense capabilities. The fighter squadron grew to 73 aircraft and the dive-bomber and torpedo-bomber squadrons were reduced to 15 aircraft each. Such a large fighter squadron soon proved too unwieldy, so in January 1945 it was split into two units – a fighter and a fighter-bomber squadron, each with 36 aircraft. In 1945, two carrier air groups sent their dive-bomber squadrons ashore and operated 93 fighters and 15 torpedo-bombers instead.

US NAVY TORPEDO-BOMBER

The essential ingredient allowing carrier air groups to sink battleships was an effective torpedo attack component, and for much of the war they lacked this capability. At the time of the Pearl Harbor raid the US Navy's standard torpedo-bomber was the TBD-1 Devastator. When introduced in 1937, it was the first widely used carrier-based monoplane as well as the first all-metal naval aircraft. A modern design, it featured a totally enclosed cockpit and power-actuated folding wings. However, by the start of the Pacific War, the Devastator was the most obsolete aircraft in the carrier air

This May 1, 1942 view of the port side of a TBM-1 Avenger shows the bulky profile of the aircraft to full advantage. The position for each of the three crewmen can also be seen (the gunner is seated inside the ball turret), and the ball turret and ventral guns are clearly evident. (Real War Photos)

group. This fact was rammed home during the Battle of Midway in June 1942, when the TBD squadrons involved in this pivotal action were all but annihilated by IJN A6M Zero-sen fighters. Fortunately, the Devastator's replacement was waiting in the wings.

Work on a successor for the TBD had officially commenced in March 1939 when the US Navy issued its design requirements for a new carrier-capable torpedo-bomber. The requirements included a top speed of 260 knots (300mph), a 3,000-mile range, an internal weapons bay and an onboard armament of two forward and two aft-firing machine guns (one of the latter in a powered turret developed by Grumman engineer Oscar Olsen in collaboration with the General Electric company). Two firms responded with proposals, although the XTBF-1 design by Grumman, a long-time supplier of aircraft to the US Navy, was clearly superior. In December 1940, 286 aircraft were ordered.

Development of the TBF proceeded quickly, and it was remarkably trouble-free. In a period of just five weeks the Grumman team, under chief engineer Bob Hall, roughed out the design. Working with the proven Wright R-2600-8 radial engine, which could develop 1,700hp at takeoff, the design met all requirements. It was not a handsome aircraft, with its portly fuselage, large angular wing and distinctive tail, but it was sound. The TBF's shape earned it the nickname "The Turkey". As demanded by the US Navy, Grumman was able to fit a powered turret with a 0.50in. Browning M-2 machine gun at the rear of the cockpit, a second 0.30in. Browning M-1919 weapon in the rear ventral area of the fuselage and a single 0.30in. gun in the nose (on early model aircraft). The latter weapon was soon replaced by two wing-mounted 0.50in. M-2s.

Perhaps the TBF's most notable design feature was the new "compound angle" wing-folding mechanism created by Grumman so as to allow the US Navy to maximize storage space on aircraft carriers. This reduced the TBF's 54ft 2in. wingspan to just 18ft 4in., the new folding wing mechanism subsequently being used by the F4F-4 Wildcat and F6F Hellcat.

The prototype took to the air for the first time on August 7, 1941, and although it crashed on November 28 after making many successful flights, the test program suffered only a slight delay. Need for the aircraft was extreme, with the war underway

OVERLEAF This TBM-3 was assigned to VT-84, embarked in USS *Bunker Hill* (CV-17) with Carrier Air Group 84 from January to June 1945. During this period the squadron participated in the Tokyo strikes in February and helped sink *Yamato* on April 7, 1945. The distinctive yellow nose band was applied to VT-84 aircraft as a special recognition measure for the first Tokyo strikes, and it was retained for a number of weeks afterward. The vertical arrow on the aircraft's tail and atop its starboard wing was the "G symbol" for Carrier Air Group 84.

TBM-3 AVENGER

40ft 0in.

16ft 5in.

54ft 2in.

and only a small number of Devastators available. The first production examples of the new aircraft, called the Avenger, were produced in January 1942. By November of that same year production surpassed 100 aircraft per month at the Grumman plant, but requirements still exceeded supply. To meet this demand, the Eastern Aircraft Division of General Motors began building the Avenger in late 1942 – such aircraft were designated the TBM. In all, 2,291 TBFs and 7,546 TBMs were completed.

The first fleet unit to receive the Avenger was Torpedo Squadron (VT) 8 in April 1942. It subsequently gave the TBF its combat debut in June 1942 during the Battle of Midway when six aircraft were employed in a land-based role. As previously mentioned, Midway also saw the end of the Devastator's combat service, so the TBF was now the sole US Navy torpedo-bomber. By any measure, the Avenger must be seen as a huge success, and it duly became the most produced naval strike aircraft in history. It was reliable in service and proved able to take tremendous punishment. It was also versatile, since it could perform in both the torpedo attack and conventional bomber roles. The only problem with the aircraft was its principal weapon, the unreliable Mark 13 air-launched torpedo.

Pilots from VT-8 inspect one of the first TBF-1s delivered to NAS Norfolk in January–February 1942. This elevated view clearly shows off the bombardier's position behind the pilot. The second cockpit also had flight controls, which were deleted as unnecessary after the 50th production aircraft. Many of VT-8's early Avengers were returned to the factory for modifications to improve functioning of the wing-folding mechanisms, thus preventing the squadron's scheduled deployment to the Pacific on board the carrier USS *Hornet* (CV-8). (Grumman)

US NAVY DIVE-BOMBER

The US Navy went to war with a proven dive-bomber in the form of the Douglas SBD Dauntless. Given the problems with the Devastator and the Mark 13 torpedo, the Dauntless was the US Navy's only consistently effective carrier-based offensive weapon in 1942–43. At the Battle of Midway, the Dauntless was the indispensable weapon for American victory. It was a dependable aircraft, easy to fly and a stable platform for dive-bombing. It did have deficiencies since it could carry only a maximum of 1,000lbs of bombs externally. The SBD was also relatively slow.

Even before hostilities commenced in the Pacific, the US Navy was working to upgrade its dive-bombing capability with a more modern aircraft. The specification for a new carrier scout bomber issued in August 1938 called for a stressed-skin monoplane with an internal weapons bay able to take a 1,000lb bomb and other stores. The aircraft had to be stressed for dive-bombing and capable of carrier operations, with folding wings, an arrestor hook and catapult hooks. Two of the aircraft had to fit on a single 40ft x 48ft carrier elevator. The crew was set as two. In order to surpass the range of the Dauntless, a large amount of fuel was to be carried. The specified engine was the Wright R-2600 14-cylinder Cyclone, which would

The Douglas SBD Dauntless remained in carrier service until mid-1944, when it was finally replaced by the Helldiver. The Dauntless was rugged and easy to fly, and, most importantly proved to be an accurate platform for dive-bombing. It did suffer from range and speed limitations, however. In this photograph, the launch officer has raised his checkered flag, ready to give the SBD pilot from VB-5 the signal to commence his deck-run takeoff from *Yorktown*. (Naval History and Heritage Command, Photo Archives, Naval Subject Collection)

provide enough power for a top speed much greater than the Dauntless.

The team at Curtiss in Buffalo, New York, had a long history of building dive-bombers, and took up this new challenge under project engineer Raymond C. Blaylock. The primary design problem was producing an aircraft big enough for an internal weapons bay and large fuel capacity, but small enough to meet the requirement to fit two on a carrier elevator. This conundrum was the cause of a long and painful gestation period. However, such was the US Navy's confidence in Curtiss and so great was the need for a new dive-bomber that an order for 370 of the new SB2C-1 aircraft was placed on May 15, 1939, *before* the aircraft had made its first flight.

The XSB2C-1 prototype was rolled out on December 13, 1940, and flown for the first time five days later. In early February the aircraft crashed when its Wright engine suddenly quit. The prototype was rebuilt, but was lost for good on December 21, 1941, when the aircraft's wing failed in flight. By then its main problems had been clearly exposed – directional instability, structural weakness, and inadequate power. The program had a high priority, however, so the designers and engineers at Curtiss pressed on.

The first flight by a production aircraft took place on June 30, 1942. Testing of the SB2C was hampered by a prohibition on high-speed dives because of structural problems, while weight increases reduced the top speed from 320 to 280 knots. Hundreds of changes were made to the design to fix problems, and these slowed production. Although the first delivery to a fleet squadron was made on December 15, 1942, when naval aviators got their hands on the aircraft, now named the Helldiver, it was not even close to being suitable for carrier operations. Almost all those who had the opportunity to fly both the Dauntless and the Helldiver preferred the much more forgiving SBD. When the SB2C was finally put aboard carriers in early 1943, it was judged unsuitable for "blue water" operations, prompting Curtiss engineers to make another round of modifications. Aviators called the aircraft "The Beast" because of its handling characteristics.

An SB2C-1 "on the wing" in February 1943. When "The Beast" went to sea on board *Yorktown* three months later, the aircraft's atrocious slow-speed handling characteristics and low serviceability forced a return to the proven Dauntless so as not to slow the carrier's deployment to the Pacific. (Naval History and Heritage Command, Photo Archives, Naval Subject Collection)

By early 1944 many of the problems had finally been rectified, and the SB2C-3 version was approved for fleet service. Eventually, 30 US Navy squadrons used the aircraft in combat, flying from 13 different fleet carriers – Helldivers were never part of carrier air groups assigned to light carriers.

Despite the numerous modifications made by Curtiss during an excessively long gestation period, the Helldiver came up short of expectations in respect to it greatly surpassing the performance of the Dauntless. However, after its developmental problems were overcome, it did prove to be an accurate dive-bomber, and demonstrated an ability to take damage. With the emphasis on fighters late in the war, and with the new F6F Hellcat and F4U Corsair proving capable of performing well in the fighter-bomber role, the Helldiver played a decreasing role in carrier operations. In fact, by the end of the war, some carrier air groups had eliminated the aircraft altogether.

Tailhooks locked down, a section of two SB2Cs from VB-17 maintain station in the landing pattern over *Bunker Hill* whilst squadronmates land back on board following the Rabaul raid of November 11, 1943. (Capt Robert B. Wood)

The introduction of the SB2C-3 with its larger engine and other modifications largely solved the problems that had plagued the aircraft earlier in its career. This flak-damaged Helldiver from VB-15, embarked in *Essex*, was involved in Carrier Air Group 15's first combat strikes (on Marcus Island) in May 1944. (Jim Sullivan)

YAMATO-CLASS BATTLESHIP

Yamato and *Musashi* were the largest battleships ever built. They were designed without any restriction in order to achieve a qualitative overmatch against battleships fielded by any potential foreign competitor. As such, they had the highest degree of protection possible. This was to be tested late in the war when these ships met not an American battleship, but clouds of American carrier aircraft.

Throughout the interwar period, a series of naval treaties forced the IJN to continually seek ways to overcome its position of numerical inferiority against the US Navy. The approach employed by the Japanese was to create ships with superior firepower and speed. Protection was not the foremost IJN design priority, usually

SB2C-3 HELLDIVER

36ft 9in.

14ft 9in.

49ft 9in.

being secondary to the design factors just mentioned. Only with ships able to employ greater firepower at superior ranges could the IJN see a way out of its numerical inferiority in any fleet clash against the US Navy.

The collapse of the naval treaty system gave the Japanese a chance to take their preference for superior ships to new heights. Without any naval treaties in place, the US Navy would be free to build at a pace that the IJN could never match. The Japanese answer was to build ships so powerful that the IJN would possess a qualitative advantage. In December 1934, Japan announced that it would renounce all naval treaties then in effect, although the IJN did not actually do so until January 1937. Nevertheless, it made plans to create a class of super battleships that would secure the necessary qualitative edge over the US Navy. In 1934, the Naval General Staff approved plans for the construction of four super battleships. Authorization of the first two super battleships, *Yamato* and *Musashi*, was provided in July 1936 and the final two ships were approved in September 1939.

DESIGN AND CONSTRUCTION

In October 1934 the Bureau of Naval Construction was directed by the Naval General Staff to start design work on the new class of super battleships. The first design was completed in March 1935, followed by an additional 22 before the final plan was accepted in July 1936. Just two months later a major redesign commenced when it was discovered that the high-powered diesel engines intended for the new ship were faulty – turbine engines would have to be used instead. The revised design was ready in March 1937.

Japanese naval architects had been challenged by the Naval General Staff to come up with a design that met the IJN's requirements for a ship with nine 18.1in. guns, armor capable of withstanding 18in. shellfire, underwater protection capable of defeating torpedoes with a 660lb warhead, a top speed of 27 knots and a cruising range of 8,000 miles at 18 knots. To accomplish this, the designers determined that the super battleship needed a displacement of no less than 69,000 tons.

Yamato was duly built in Kure after the dock there had been deepened and gantry cranes strengthened to handle the ship's enormous armor plates. *Musashi* was built at the Mitsubishi shipyard at Nagasaki. Expansion of this facility required that the slipway be extended some 50ft into a hillside. Extreme security precautions taken during the ships' construction were successful in denying US Naval Intelligence an accurate assessment of the super battleship's size and capabilities throughout the war. In 1939, two more Yamato-class ships were authorized. Although the first of these was christened *Shinano*, the second was never named. *Shinano* was intended to be completed with a different armor scheme, and it was to

This is another photograph that was taken of *Yamato* during its sea trials in October 1941. This view of the super battleship, taken from its port quarter whilst making high speed, would have been similar to the perspective of a torpedo-bomber pilot as he bored in for an attack in his TBM. (Naval History and Heritage Command, Photo Archives, Naval Subject Collection)

The bow area of *Musashi*, photographed from the forward superstructure during sea trials in June 1942. The uncluttered deck would be changed during the war following the addition of large numbers of 25mm antiaircraft guns. (Naval History and Heritage Command, Photo Archives, Naval Subject Collection)

This view from *Musashi*'s bow shows the size of the forward 18.1in. turrets and the imposing superstructure. The triple 6.1in. beam turrets can also be seen. These were removed in April 1944 to provide more space for 25mm antiaircraft guns in an attempt to boost the ship's protection from air attack. (Naval History and Heritage Command, Photo Archives, Naval Subject Collection)

have been equipped with the new Type 98 4in./65 antiaircraft gun. After Midway, the IJN decided to complete the ship as an aircraft carrier. Ready for service by late 1944, *Shinano* was sunk by a US Navy submarine on November 28 during its first voyage. The fourth Yamato-class ship was only 30 percent complete when work was halted in November 1941.

The hull of the Yamato class had a very broad beam of 127.7ft, with overall length being 839ft. Draft was relatively shallow for a ship with such a large displacement. Nevertheless, when it was fully loaded the draft was still 35.4ft, which meant that several harbors had to be dredged before they could accommodate the super battleship. Finally, a new feature seen on both ships was a giant bulbous bow that had been shown during tests to reduce hydrodynamic drag.

PROTECTION

As demanded in the design specifications, the armor scheme was of such a scale that it provided the class with an unparalleled degree of protection. Armor was laid out on an "all or nothing" principle, with all armor being placed in the central main citadel to protect vital machinery and magazine spaces. The bow and stern sections of the ship were unarmored. In order to minimize the portions of the ship that were to be protected, the super battleship was designed with an unprecedented beam instead of a long narrow hull design. This reduced the area of the hull that had to be protected to just 53.3 percent of its waterline depth.

Yamato was the most heavily protected ship ever built, with its armor weighing 22,534 tons in total – 33.1 percent of the warship's design displacement. The armored citadel featured a main defensive belt of 16in. inclined at 20 degrees, half of which was below the waterline. The lower armor belt was just under 11 inches thick where it protected the magazines and 8 inches thick surrounding the machinery spaces. The ends of the armored citadel were covered by two transverse 11.8in. bulkheads. Deck armor was between 7.9 and 9.1 inches thick, and it was calculated to be capable of withstanding armor-piercing bombs of up to 2,200lbs (1,000kg) dropped from 3,280ft (1,000 meters). The fronts of the turret barbettes were covered by 21.5 inches of armor plate, with the sides covered by 16 inches, both specially hardened. The three main turrets featured some 26 inches of armor on their face, 10 inches on the sides, 9.5 inches in the rear and almost 11 inches on the roofs. The conning tower was covered by a maximum of 19.7 inches of steel.

Additional protective features included thick armor around the two steering engine compartments, while the floors of the magazines boasted two to three inches of armor plate as a precaution against mines or torpedoes. The

uptake in the stack was protected by perforated armor plates of 15 inches, while its inclined surface was protected by two inches of armor that would detonate bombs before they hit the perforated plate.

The anti-torpedo defense system relied primarily on the placement of a side blister with void compartments. The depth of the blister varied from 8.5ft in the area of Turret No. 2 to a maximum of 16.4ft amidships.

DAMAGE CONTROL MEASURES

Yamato's hull was divided into 1,147 watertight compartments – 1,065 below the armor deck and 82 above. The reserve buoyancy was 57,450 tons, which was 80 percent of the trial displacement. If the bow or stern sections were flooded, it was assessed that the ship could maintain stability until the list reached 20 degrees. It was also believed that the ship would remain functional even if the freeboard forward went from the usual 33ft to only 15ft.

The flooding and pumping system was designed to correct the list of the first torpedo hit within five minutes of being activated. By flooding the control tanks on the opposite of the ship, a 13.8-degree list could be corrected. A further 4.5 degrees could be corrected by pumping fuel to the opposite fuel tanks. In this manner, two torpedo hits could be compensated for in 30 minutes and three hits in 60 minutes. Four torpedo hits would result in a list of only 5 degrees after completion of damage control measures.

PROPULSION

The ship's enormous beam allowed the four main turbines and their boilers to be placed side-by-side instead of in tandem along the length of the hull. This reduced the area that had to be armored to protect the machinery. The ship had 12 Kampon 13,500 shaft horsepower (shp) boilers arranged in three rows of four, with each boiler in a separate room. The four Kampon geared turbines were arranged in four separate spaces, with two outboard and two inboard on each side. This provided a total of 150,000shp to the four propeller shafts, and these allowed the ship to meet the design speed of 27.5 knots. *Yamato* was reported to have made in excess of 28 knots in June 1942. Maneuverability was excellent through the use of a main and an auxiliary rudder. The ship's tactical diameter was a fairly compact 698 yards. A small heeling angle even at extreme degrees of rudder at high speed meant that the Yamato-class ships were good platforms for gunnery.

ARMAMENT

The centerpiece of the Yamato-class design was the main armament of 18.1in. guns – the largest weapons ever placed on a battleship. Each gun weighed 162 tons, and the rotating components of the triple turret totaled 2,774 tons – equivalent in weight to a fleet destroyer. Each gun fired an enormous 3,219lb projectile. The rate of fire was 1.5 rounds per minute. Secondary armament was comprised of four triple turrets with 6.1in. guns. These were placed forward and aft and one on each beam. The IJN had hoped that these turrets would

This is a close-up of *Musashi*'s superstructure in June 1943, viewed from alongside its 18.1in. Turret No. 1. The object atop the superstructure is the fire control director for the 18.1in. main battery guns, and below it is the 49.2ft-wide main battery rangefinder. The level below the rangefinder contained the Air Defense Combat Station, from where the captain would direct the ship's maneuvers during air attack. The device on the face of the superstructure is a navigation rangefinder, while the instruments to either side are Type 95 fire control directors for the 25mm guns. (Naval History and Heritage Command, Photo Archives, Naval Subject Collection)

also augment the ship's anti-air protection, but they proved inadequate in that role and eventually resulted in the removal of the beam turrets.

Antiaircraft protection was typical of other battleships designed in the 1930s. Long-range protection was provided by 12 5in. guns mounted in six twin mounts. These were grouped amidships, three per side, and placed above the beam 6.1in. triple turrets. As designed, the Yamato class was provided with 24 25mm guns in eight triple mounts and four 13mm guns on the bridge tower.

The Yamato class featured extensive facilities for handling aircraft, with two 59ft catapults being fitted on the quarterdeck. There was a hangar deck located below the main deck that could handle up to seven floatplanes, although the normal number embarked was usually only three or four.

YAMATO CLASS – AN ASSESSMENT

As formidable as the design for the Yamato class appeared on paper, there were problems. The armor distribution scheme proved to be faulty, with the entire bow and stern sections relying on compartmentation only. However, the compartments in these areas of the ship were too large for this to work. Damage inflicted in either area invariably translated into flooding and a list, with the pumping system being unable to cope with excessive water levels in the bow and/or stern.

An even larger problem was the joint between the armor of the upper and lower side belts. The solution – using two different types of rivets – was simply inadequate. Because these lacked adequate transverse strength against the shearing effects of an explosion, like that of a torpedo, they constituted a critical weakness that could threaten the integrity of the entire armored citadel. The effectiveness of the torpedo bulges was also reduced since they contained only air. They would have been more effective had the bulges been filled with some sort of liquid, like fuel oil, in order to absorb some of the energy from an explosion. The lack of an agent in the bulge to absorb energy meant that the main belt facing the inside of the bulge was exposed to most of the blast.

This problem was demonstrated by a single hit on *Yamato* from a torpedo launched by the submarine USS *Skate* (SS-305) on December 25, 1943. The weapon struck its starboard quarter, creating a hole some 80ft long in the area of the aft main battery director, the aft 6.1-in. turret and the forward part of Turret No. 3. The integrity of the armored citadel was compromised and flooding of Turret No. 3's magazine occurred, with 3,000 tons of water entering

Yamato under construction at the IJN's Kure naval base on September 20, 1941. The aircraft carrier *Hosho* is moored to the right of the super battleship, while the supply ship *Mamiya* can be seen in the center distance. (Japanese National Archive)

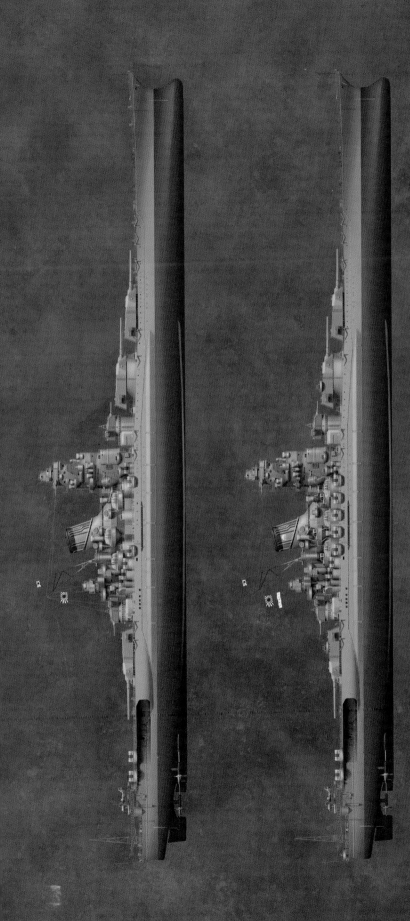

MUSASHI (left)

This profile shows *Musashi* as it appeared in October 1944 when the ship was sunk in the Sibuyan Sea. The ship presents a graceful and powerful appearance dominated by its three triple 18.1in. gun turrets, raked stack and large superstructure. Not readily apparent is *Musashi*'s large antiaircraft battery of 130 25mm guns arranged in 35 triple mounts (most clustered amidships) and 25 single mounts (positioned on the weather deck fore and aft). These light weapons were augmented by a battery of 12 5in. Type 89 guns (three twin mounts can be seen amidships near the stack) and the two 6.1in. turrets of the secondary battery. Although this array of weapons could throw up impressive volumes of fire, it proved to be ineffective when it came to defending the ship from a sustained aerial attack.

YAMATO (right)

This profile shows *Yamato* in April 1945 at the time of its loss in the East China Sea. The ship retains its basic appearance from its early war configuration, with the principal exception of a greatly augmented antiaircraft suite. *Yamato*'s final antiaircraft fit included an astounding 152 25mm guns. These were arrayed in 50 triple mounts, many of which can be seen in this starboard view. After the battle of Leyte Gulf, *Yamato* received another nine triple mounts, most of which were fitted amidships on the outer edge of the weather deck. These mounts were provided with a new type of shield — 16 other mounts were provided with a shield design from 1941. The shields were necessary to protect the gun crews from the blast pressure created by the nearby 5in. gun mounts when they were fired. *Yamato* carried 12 Type 89 twin mounts, with the lower ones being provided with blast shields. The chrysanthemum crest on the stack was carried only for *Ten-Go*, as was the samurai banner below the national ensign. The upper flag is a vice admiral's ensign, which was flown for the task force commander, Vice Admiral Ito Seiichi.

Yamato (left) and *Musashi* (right) moored in Truk Lagoon sometime during 1943. Both ships spent the majority of that year at anchor here, the IJN's principal Central Pacific base, without seeing any action. (Naval History and Heritage Command, Photo Archives, Naval Subject Collection)

the ship. A single torpedo had defeated *Yamato*'s underwater defenses.

When the side protection system failed, the armored citadel was compromised. The maximum width of the anti-torpedo bulge around the machinery spaces was only 16.7ft – well below that of foreign battleships designed during the same period. The lack of depth was compounded by the fact that the bulge was tied to the main belt armor. In 1943, the US Navy introduced a new explosive, Torpex, with twice the destructive power of TNT. This rendered all the calculations of *Yamato*'s designers obsolete. While the ship's sheer size and heavy armor made it difficult to destroy, *Yamato*'s anti-torpedo defenses were the weakest part of its design. As it turned out, they were the part of the battleship's protection scheme that was to be tested the most during the war.

Despite the weaknesses noted in this chapter, the Yamato class was an undeniable triumph for Japanese warship designers and builders. The warship that entered service in late 1941 was the largest, most powerfully armed and the best protected ship in the world. Unfortunately for the Japanese, the era of the battleship was coming to a close. Just days before *Yamato* was commissioned on December 16, 1941, the IJN had amply demonstrated the power of naval aircraft by sinking five US Navy battleships in Pearl Harbor. If there remained doubt that battleships could survive at sea against naval air power, this was erased on December 10 when the modern British battleship HMS *Prince of Wales* and the aged battlecruiser HMS *Repulse* were sunk off the coast of Malaya by Japanese aircraft.

During the design phase of the Yamato class, their main threat was believed to be other battleships, not aircraft. In fact, the IJN's super battleships never engaged another battleship in combat, but by 1944 they faced an intense air threat that they were not designed to cope with. The eventual nemesis of the IJN's super battleships was a relatively primitive tool when the ships were designed, and it was impossible to foresee the rapid technological advances of carrier aircraft and the subsequent domination of naval air power. When completed, *Yamato* may have been the symbol of the IJN and the entire nation, but it was also obsolete.

TECHNICAL SPECIFICATIONS

TBF/TBM AVENGER

By 1944, the only torpedo-bomber in US Navy service was the TBF/TBM Avenger. Primary variants of the Avenger are outlined below.

TBF-1

The first production model built by Grumman, the TBF-1 was armed with one 0.30in. machine gun mounted in the cowling, in addition to the ventral 0.30in. weapon and the turret equipped with a 0.50in. machine gun. The TBF-1 (1,526 built) was also constructed by Eastern Aircraft as the TBM-1 (550 built).

TBF-1B

US Navy designation for Lend–Lease aircraft supplied to the Royal Navy.

TBF/TBM-1C

Introduced in 1943 (2,336 built), with several improvements including replacement of the cowling 0.30in. weapon with two wing-mounted 0.50in. machine guns and the addition of

With its 0.50in. ball turret machine gun and a ventral position with a 0.30in. weapon, the Avenger possessed the means to defend itself against enemy fighters attacking from the rear. Flying in formation increased the aircraft's defensive capabilities. These early-build TBF-1s boast typical colors and markings for 1942 – blue-gray uppersurfaces and medium gray undersides, with the national insignia (without the red center) in six positions. (Grumman)

This TBM/TBF-1C Avenger from VT-30 is seen during a training flight in the fall of 1943, prior to embarking for the Pacific on board USS *Monterey* (CVL-26) with the rest of Light Carrier Air Group 30. Each Independence-class light carrier air group included nine Avengers and as many as 24 F6Fs – in the case of VT-30, its Avengers shared CVL-26's modest flightdeck with Hellcats from VF-30. The -1C variant could be recognized by the position and angle of the radio antenna mast positioned above the canopy. (Naval History and Heritage Command, Photo Archives, Naval Subject Collection)

A TBM-3 of VT-6, embarked in USS *Hancock* (CV-19), flies over ships of TF 58 off Okinawa in the spring of 1945. Assigned to Carrier Air Group 6 along with VF-6 (F6F-5s), VBF-6 (F4U-4s) and VB-6 (SB2C-3/3Es and -4/4Es), VT-6 was involved in the April 7, 1945 action that resulted in the sinking of *Yamato*. However, CV-19's strike group (consisting of Helldivers and Avengers) launched late and then got lost, so it never made an attack on the super battleship. (National Archives)

bulletproof glass in the turret. Later production aircraft had four launch rails for 5in. rockets beneath each wing.

TBF/TBM-1D

This was a conversion of TBF/TBM-1 and -1Cs into night-capable aircraft through the addition of a radome containing ASD-1 radar on the leading edge of the starboard wing.

TBM-3

This was the most-produced version of the Avenger, and it featured the more powerful Wright R-2600-20 engine rated at 1,900hp. TBM-3s were exclusively built by Eastern Aircraft, some 4,011 being completed. It was hoped that the addition of the more powerful engine would increase performance, but this was negated by the aircraft's increased weight.

TBM-3D

Night bomber version of the TBM-3 with radome containing ASD-1 radar on the leading edge of the starboard wing.

TBM-3E

This variant (646 built) was introduced late in the war and featured a stronger airframe, search radar and no ventral gun.

TBM-3 AVENGER ARMAMENT

The TBM-3 Avenger was well armed, being able to both defend itself against Japanese fighters and effectively conduct strafing missions. This view shows the two wing-mounted 0.50in. Browning M-2 machine guns, each of which had a magazine holding 335 rounds. Providing the aircraft with a powered turret (developed by Grumman engineer Oscar Olsen in collaboration with the General Electric company) for self-defense was a prime design consideration. In the turret was another 0.50in. machine gun, along with a magazine holding 400 rounds. Not shown here is the ventral 0.30in. Browning M-1919 machine gun with 5000 rounds. Once combined with the ordnance load of 2,000lbs of stores in the internal bomb-bay and eight wing-mounted 5-inch rockets, the Avenger became a formidable offensive platform.

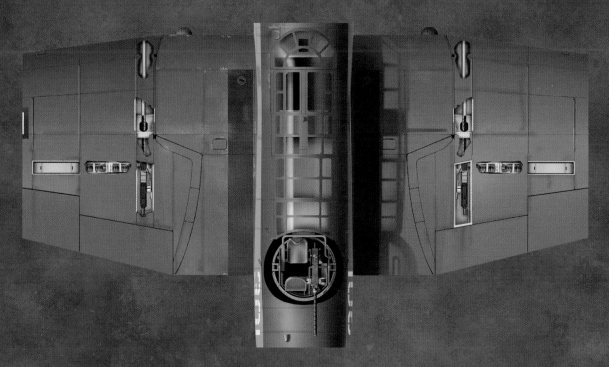

TBM-3 Avenger Specification

Powerplant	1,900hp Wright R-2600-20 Cyclone
Dimensions	
Span	54ft 2in
Length	40ft
Height	16ft 5in
Wing area	490.02 sq ft
Weight	
Empty	10,843lb
Loaded	17,893lb
Performance	
Max speed	267mph at 16,000ft
Range	1,130 miles with torpedo and 1,920 miles without

Rate of climb	2,060ft per minute
Service ceiling	23,400ft
Armament	One Mark 13 torpedo or 2,000lb of bombs or depth charges
	Two wing-mounted 0.50in Browning M-2 machine guns, each with 335 rounds per gun
	One turret-mounted 0.50in Browning M-2 machine gun with 400 rounds
	One ventral 0.30in. Browning M-1919 machine gun with 5000 rounds

MARK 13 TORPEDO

A TBF-1 dropping a Mark 13 torpedo during exercises in October 1942. At this point in the war the Mark 13 was unreliable, and Avengers were often loaded with bombs instread to attack Japanese shipping. (Naval History and Heritage Command)

To be effective, a torpedo-bomber obviously needs a reliable weapon. Unfortunately for the US Navy, this proved to be a difficult problem to overcome. Work on its first aerial torpedo had started in 1917, with the Type D commencing test drops in 1918. Two years later, the weapon was replaced by the larger Mark 7 aerial torpedo. Its Mod B version had a 319lb warhead, although this proved to be so fragile in service that the weapon had to be launched at a precise attitude and at speeds below 80 knots. If not, the Mod B would sink or run erratically. Nevertheless, the Mark 7 was the standard US Navy aerial torpedo for the remainder of the 1920s and into the 1930s.

When this weapon was finally deemed to be unsatisfactory in service, design work began on a new torpedo that could be launched at greater speeds and which had greater reliability. Development of the weapon (designated the Mark 13) commenced in 1930, and by 1932 test runs had begun. The first aerial tests took place in the spring of 1935, with 23 drops being made between May 27 and October 1 – a further 20 were expended in 1936. Early results were good, and when the Mark 13 entered service in 1938, fleet tests confirmed that the weapon was reliable and could be launched at altitudes of between 40ft and 90ft and at a speed of 100 knots.

A Mark 13 torpedo is carefully lined up prior to being winched into the bomb-bay of an Avenger 'somewhere in the Pacific' in 1942–43. Note the crewman standing on the wing holding a Yagi-style row antenna from the ASB radar system. Late production TBF-1s were equipped with long-wave ASB radar, with a Yagi-style row antenna under each wing, to give them a foul-weather attack capability. The radio operator handled the radar. Although ASB was a primitive system, it proved to be more than adequate when it came to finding a ship-sized target at moderate ranges. (National Archives)

The original Mark 13 Mod 0 (of which 156 were produced) was replaced by the Mod 1 in 1940, the new torpedo having a different rudder-propeller arrangement – the Mod 0 had a rail-type tail in which the propellers were in front of the rudder, whereas the Mod 1 was fitted with a conventional tail. At this point the weapon became chronically unreliable, the torpedo tending to veer left after entering the water and running deeper than it was set for. After much corrective work had been carried out, the Bureau of Ordnance thought that these problems had been fixed. However, it could not find a way to increase the speed at which the weapon could be launched. The 30-knot top speed of the torpedo itself was also major a problem since many of the targets the weapon was fired against could simply outrun it.

Aviation ordnancemen wheel Mark 13 torpedoes across *Hornet*'s flightdeck to be loaded aboard TBF-1Cs (out of shot)of VT-2 for the "Mission Beyond Darkness", which was flown on June 20, 1944. (US Navy)

Despite the torpedo being recognized as an inferior weapon of dubious reliability, the US Navy's carrier-based torpedo-bomber squadron still went to war equipped with the Mark 13.

It took two more years to completely solve the problem of the Mark 13's reliability. This was finally achieved by adding a shroud ring to the tail of the torpedo, which reduced its erratic behavior when the weapon entered the water. Another innovation was the addition of a water trip valve that ignited the torpedo for running only after it had entered the water. The final modification was a drag ring that was made of plywood and placed over the warhead. This helped absorb the shock of hitting the water, added more stability to the run and reduced the depth to which the torpedo would plunge.

These modifications were ready by late 1944, which meant that when the US Navy faced the IJN's all-out attempt in October 1944 to repel the American invasion of the Philippines, the Avenger finally had a reliable weapon. When opposed by heavy antiaircraft fire, the Avenger could drop its weapon at close to the aircraft's top speed of 270mph and at a more survivable altitude of up to 800ft.

Mark 13 Aerial Torpedo Specification		
	Mod 0	Mod 1
Dimensions		
Length	13ft 5in.	13ft 9in.
Diameter	22in.	22in.
Weight	1,949lb	2,216lb
Warhead	392lb of TNT or 404lb TPX	603lb of TNT, 606lb of TPX or 600lb of HBX
Speed	30 knots	30 knots
Propulsion	Steam	Steam
Range	5,700 yards	5,700 yards

Six SB2C-1s are seen on a training flight in the United States in December 1943. They may be from VB-20, which had only recently been formed at San Diego at the time with 18 SBD-5s and nine SB2C-1s. This unit, now fully equipped with SB2C-3s and embarked in *Enterprise*, played a key role in the sinking of *Musashi* on October 24, 1944. (Jim Sullivan)

SB2C HELLDIVER

After the Helldiver's design and production problems were overcome, Curtiss went on to build 5,516 examples of the aircraft, with the last one being delivered in October 1945. The principal variants of the Helldiver were as follows.

SB2C-1

This was the basic production aircraft, which made its maiden flight on June 30, 1942, powered by a Wright R-2600-8 engine that produced a maximum of 1,700hp. The SB2C-1's first carrier trials were disastrous, prompting a series of modifications. The aircraft eventually made its combat debut (with VB-17, flying from USS *Bunker Hill* (CV-17)) in November 1943. The SB2C-1C was the main production variant of the "Dash 1", incorporating the many modifications required to make the aircraft carrier-capable. It also had the twin 0.50in. machine guns in each wing replaced by a single 20mm Mk 2 cannon. Total production numbered 978 aircraft.

A fine study of an SB2C-1C from VB-1, showing the rear gunner's position with its twin 0.30in. machine guns. The aerial under the port wing is for the ASB radar. Embarked in *Yorktown* from May to August 1944, VB-1 lost nine of 14 aircraft sent to attack the IJN's Mobile Fleet on June 20, 1944, although all 18 downed aircrew were recovered. (Naval History and Heritage Command, Photo Archives, Naval Subject Collection)

SB2C-2

This was an experimental seaplane version of the Helldiver that never entered production.

SB2C-3

This was the first version of the aircraft to see widespread combat service, with 1,112 being built. The principal problem with the Helldiver was that it was underpowered for its size. The new version was given the upgraded Wright R-2600-20 engine that developed 1,900hp, increasing the aircraft's maximum speed to 294mph and giving it a slightly better range. The SB2C-3 was fitted with a new four-bladed propeller. Late in its production run, new perforated dive brakes were installed that helped alleviate problems with buffeting when diving and improved low-speed handling. Some aircraft were fitted with the AN/APS-4 airborne intercept radar in an underwing bulge to replace the standard ASB sea-search radar, these Helldivers being designated SB2C-3Es.

SB3C-3 HELLDIVER ARMAMENT

The SB2C-3 largely solved the problems that gave the "Beast" its earlier bad reputation. This view shows the Helldiver's armament, which included two wing-mounted 20mm Mk 2 cannon, each with 800 rounds. The rear gunner was charged with the operation of the aircraft's principal defensive armament of two 0.30in. Browning M-1919 machine guns on a flexible mount, which could be trained to either side of the aircraft. Each gun had 2,000 rounds available. The Helldiver could also carry up to 2,000lbs of ordnance, although its usual load was two 500lb bombs, a single 1,000lb bomb or depth charges for antisubmarine operations

SB2C-3 Helldiver Specification	
Powerplant	1,900hp Wright R-2600-20 Cyclone
Dimensions	
Span	49ft 9in.
Length	36ft 9in.
Height	14ft 9in
Wing area	422 sq ft
Weight	
Empty	10,114lb
Loaded	16,800lb
Performance	
Max speed	294mph at 12,400ft
Range	1,200 miles with 1,000lb bomb-load
Rate of climb	1,800ft per minute
Ceiling	29,100ft
Armament	1,000lb of bombs or depth charges
	Two 20mm Mk 2 cannon, each with 800 rounds
	Two 0.30in. Browning M-1919 machine guns, each with 2,000 rounds

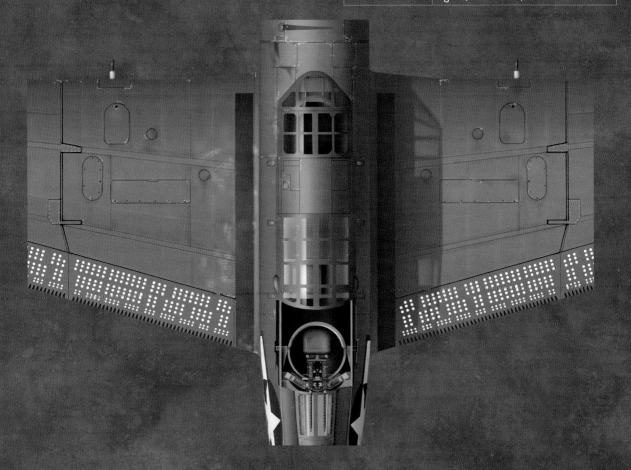

This SB2C-4 of VB-85, embarked in USS *Shangri-La* (CV-38), was photographed in August 1945. The "Dash 4" variant of the Helldiver differed from previous models by the fitment of a propeller spinner, the deletion of the small windows behind the pilot's seat and modified wing rocket launchers. By this point, the dive-bomber was becoming obsolete, as the latest generation of carrier fighter, epitomized by the F4U Corsair, could carry a comparable bomb load at higher speeds and was able to perform multiple roles. First embarked in CV-38 in November 1944, VB-85 (as part of Carrier Air Group 85) entered combat during the Okinawa campaign in April 1945. (Naval History and Heritage Command, Photo Archives, Naval Subject Collection)

SB2C-4

This variant, which kept the new dive brakes and engine, had rails fitted for eight underwing rockets. Radar-equipped aircraft were designated SB2C-4E. The most obvious difference between the "Dash 3" and "Dash 4" was that the latter aircraft had a propeller spinner. This was the most numerous Helldiver variant, with 2,045 aircraft being built.

SB2C-5

This version did not enter production until February 1945, which meant few examples reached operational squadrons prior to VJ Day. The SB2C-5 had the same R-2600-20 engine as previous variants, but capacity for an additional 35 gallons of fuel. Production totaled 970 aircraft.

YAMATO-CLASS BATTLESHIP

Yamato was commissioned on December 16, 1941. The second ship of the class, *Musashi*, entered service on August 5, 1942. When completed, both ships shared the same specifications as follows:

Length	839ft
Beam	127.7ft
Draft	35.4ft
Displacement	71,111 tons (standard)
	73,000 tons (full load)
Propulsion	12 Kanpon boilers driving four steam turbines producing 150,000shp in total

Speed	27.5 knots
Range	7,200 nautical miles at 16 knots
Protection	Main belt 16in.; transverse bulkheads 11.8in.; deck 7.9–9.1in.; barbettes 21.5in. front and 16in. side; main turrets 26in. front, 10in. side, 9.5in. rear and 10.6in. roof; conning tower 19.7in.
Armament (as built)	
Main	nine 18.1in.
Secondary	24 6.1in.
Antiaircraft	12 5in., 24 25mm and four 13mm

With the exception of augmenting their radar and antiaircraft weaponry fits, neither ship underwent any major modification during the war. While at Kure in July 1943, *Yamato* received two Type 21 radars placed atop the rangefinder on its forward superstructure. Additionally, four Type 96 25mm triple gun mounts were fitted on the weather deck, making a total of 36 25mm weapons.

Yamato's next modifications took place in February 1944 when the two beam 6.1in. turrets were removed and replaced with six twin 5in. Type 89 shielded mounts. At this time, another 24 triple 25mm mounts and 26 single 25mm guns were added. Types 22 and 13 radar were also installed. Later, between June 29 and July 8, 1944, another five 25mm triple mounts were installed. In November 1944 *Yamato* was drydocked to repair battle damage from Leyte. At this time almost all of the single 25mm mounts were removed and nine additional triple mounts added. *Yamato*'s final antiaircraft fit was an impressive 152 25mm guns in 50 triple and two single mounts.

During *Musashi*'s final fitting out in Kure, another four triple 25mm guns were added. In September 1943 two Type 21 radars were fitted, and seven months later, while in Kure for repairs for torpedo damage, *Musashi*'s two beam 6.1in. turrets were removed and replaced by a total of six 25mm triple mounts. Additional triple mounts and 25 single mounts were also added at this time, bringing the total to 115 guns — Types 22 and 13 radar were also fitted. In July 1944 the ship underwent final modifications, with another five triple 25mm mounts fitted aboard. *Musashi*'s final antiaircraft suite was thus 130 25mm guns – 35 triple and 25 single mounts.

Antiaircraft fit for Yamato-Class Battleships		
Yamato	**Type 89 5in. guns**	**Type 96 25mm guns**
12/41	12	24
7/43	12	36
4/44	24	116
7/44	24	131
4/45	24	152
Musashi	**Type 89 5in. guns**	**Type 96 25mm guns**
8/42	12	36
4/44	12	115
7/44	12	130

TYPE 89 5in. GUN

The Type 89 5in. (12.7cm) High Angle Gun was adopted in February 1932. It was a dual mount and was the standard long-range antiaircraft gun for all IJN heavy ships, including the Yamato-class battleships. The IJN was very satisfied with this weapon since it combined reliability with fairly high elevating speeds, a high muzzle velocity and large shells, which came in three types – Common, Common Type 3 (fragmentation) and Illuminating Shell B. With a well-trained crew, it had a high rate of fire. The main drawback of the weapon was its fairly short effective vertical range of only 24,272ft.

The fire control system for the Type 89 was the Type 94 High Angle Firing Control Installation. Although the Type 94 was adopted in 1934, it did not go into production for a further three years. This subsequently meant that the system was in short supply during the war. However, both Yamato-class battleships received Type 94 equipment as a matter of priority, each being fitted with two systems (*Yamato* later received two more). These were located in pairs abeam the forward superstructure and mainmast. The fire director towers fed information to a fire control room located below the armored deck. Each fire director tower had a Type 94 14.76ft stereoscopic rangefinder and four 3in. telescopes. The towers were trained electro-hydraulically and elevated manually. The towers measured the range to the target, as well as its horizontal and vertical inclination, and then sent this data to the plotting room, where an analog computer calculated a firing solution. The latter was the required elevation and deflection and shell fuze settings that the gun mounts needed to engage a target successfully.

The Type 94 had issues with tracking high-speed targets, taking some 20 seconds to detect a target and then another 10–12 seconds to produce a fire control solution. This made it simply too slow to deal with US Navy carrier aircraft. The computer-generated fire control solutions were also inaccurate. While the US Navy's 5in. gun proved to be its primary antiaircraft weapon, the IJN's mounts of the same size were ineffective in this role. This meant that the burden of air defense for the Yamato-class ships rested with the close-range 25mm antiaircraft machine gun.

The Type 89 5in. High Angle Gun was the IJN's standard long-range antiaircraft weapon during the war. Despite its satisfactory technical characteristics, it was handicapped by inferior fire control equipment and faulty doctrine. Japanese records of its employment during the air attacks on *Musashi* indicate that it was used sparingly, confirming that the system had problems tracking targets conducting dive-bombing or making torpedo attacks. (*Ships of the World* Magazine)

Type 89 5in. High Angle Gun Specification	
Muzzle velocity	2,362ft per second
Barrel life	800–1,500 rounds
Rate of fire	Maximum 14 rounds per minute Sustained 11–12 rounds per minute
Range	Maximum horizontal 14,390 yards Maximum vertical 8,830 yards Effective vertical 8,065 yards

Maximum elevation	90 degrees
Shell weight	50.6lb
Max elevating speed	12 degrees per second
Max training speed	6 degrees per second
Weight of dual mount	24.5 tons (with shield)

TYPE 96 25mm ANTIAIRCRAFT GUN

For its standard short-range antiaircraft weapon, the Japanese selected the 25mm machine gun developed by the French firm Hotchkiss. The IJN modified the French weapon by fitting a flash suppressor, and subsequently adopted it in 1936 as the Type 96 25mm Machine Gun Model 1. The 1936 version was introduced as a twin mount, but a triple was introduced in 1941 and a single mount two years later. The weapon was air-cooled. The triple mount had two electric motors – one for training and the other for elevation. These could be controlled remotely from the Type 95 director. The triple mount was crewed by nine men, including six loaders.

Four different types of rounds were provided, namely common, incendiary, armor-piercing and tracer – typically, every fourth or fifth round was a tracer. The shells were contained in 15-round magazines, which were too small to allow the weapon to be used at its maximum rate of fire. Since the magazines had to be replaced frequently, the actual rate of fire was 100-110 rounds per minute (per gun for the triple mount).

The Type 96 was controlled by the Type 95 Short-Range High-Angle Director. This was a fairly simple system that measured the speed, range and altitude of the target to provide a basic fire control solution. In theory, it could handle targets traveling at up to 560mph, but the drive control motors on the mount could not cope with such high speeds. It was inferior to comparable US Navy systems. *Yamato* had four Type 95s, which were located in pairs in front of the forward superstructure and abeam the stack. In 1944–45 a simplified Type 4 Mod 3 unit was introduced, which did not have drive control motors. Each triple mount had a back-up manual sight in case the remote-control system became inoperable. The single 25mm mounts had only open-ring sights.

The IJN's choice of the 25mm gun as its standard light antiaircraft weapon was an unfortunate selection. Even the Japanese recognized its significant shortcomings, which Included inadequate training and elevation speeds, a low sustained rate of fire and excessive blast that affected accuracy. The single mount was almost worthless since it had only an open-ring sight that could not handle high-speed targets, and the weapon itself was difficult for an average crewman to handle. Another problem was that the individual shells fired by the 25mm gun were too small to

This is a Type 96 triple 25mm mount captured on Guadalcanal in October 1942. The weapon had a number of shortcomings that ultimately made it ineffective as the IJN's standard intermediate and short-range antiaircraft mount. Note the magazines above each gun, which contained 15 rounds. The frequent requirement to change these reduced the actual rate of fire to 100–110 rounds per minute. (Naval History and Heritage Command)

knock down rugged US aircraft. The failure of the IJN to develop a larger weapon comparable to the US Navy's 40mm Bofors gun was a key factor in the increasing vulnerability of Japanese surface ships as the war progressed.

Type 96 25mm Antiaircraft Machine Gun Specification	
Muzzle velocity	2,952ft per second
Barrel life	approximately 15,000 rounds
Rate of fire	Theoretical 220–240 rounds per minute Actual 110–120 rounds per minute
Range	Maximum 3,815 yards Effective 1,635 yards
Maximum elevation	80 degrees
Shell weight	8.82oz
Max elevating speed	12 degrees per second
Max training speed	18 degrees per second
Weight of triple mount	3,960lb

TYPE 3 18.1in. INCENDIARY ANTIAIRCRAFT

The Type 3 incendiary antiaircraft shell was introduced for the Yamato-class 18.1in. main guns in 1943. These *San-Shiki* shells were filled with 996 25mm x 90mm steel tubes containing an incendiary mixture. The shells employed a time fuse, and after they burst the tubes ignited following a half-second delay and burned for five seconds. The IJN expected great results from this enormous shotgun blast, which had a radius of 397ft. There was a drawback to using these shells, however, since the copper drive bands were so poorly machined that they damaged the rifling of the gun barrels when fired. Despite looking impressive when employed, the Type 3 shell proved to be totally ineffective in service.

Yamato comes under attack on October 26, 1944 while retreating through the Sibuyan Sea. In this fine overhead photograph, taken by a B-24 Liberator from the 424th Bombardment Squadron (BS) of the 307th Bombardment Group (BG), the size of the 18.1in. main gun turrets is clearly illustrated. These weapons could fire Type 3 incendiary antiaircraft shells at high-flying bombers such as B-24s, although such rounds proved to be totally ineffective in service. (Naval History and Heritage Command)

THE STRATEGIC SITUATION

The American advance toward Japan began to pick up speed in 1944. The overall strategy called for two different routes for the advance. One was through the central Pacific under the command of Adm Chester Nimitz in his capacity as Commander in Chief Pacific Fleet and Pacific Ocean Areas. The other was through New Guinea and into the Philippines, with Gen Douglas MacArthur and his Southwest Pacific Forces taking the fight to the enemy in these areas.

In June, Nimitz's forces invaded the Marianas Islands, some 1,200 miles from Japan. In the process, the US Navy and the IJN clashed in the largest carrier battle in history when 15 American ships engaged nine Japanese "flattops". The IJN had been hoarding its strength for a "decisive" battle for some 18 months, but when it occurred, the result was far different than it had expected. The battle of the Philippine Sea resulted in a crushing defeat for the Japanese carrier force, with three "flattops" sunk and the carrier air groups of the surviving ships virtually annihilated. In the wake of such a devastating reversal, the IJN's carrier force would be unable to support Japan's next major attempt to stop the American advance. This shaped the IJN's plan for the next fleet action, and directly influenced the fate of the Yamato-class battleships.

The future focus of the American drive in the Pacific was still undecided in July 1944. Nimitz and MacArthur had different ideas on how to proceed, and inter-service rivalry demanded that neither could serve under the other. MacArthur advocated for a drive through the Philippines before attacking the Japanese Home Islands. The target date for the first landings was November 15 against Mindanao, in the southern Philippines. Nimitz, supported by his boss Adm Ernest King, Chief of Naval Operations, thought that attacking through the Philippines would be a long and costly undertaking. Instead, they proposed to capture Formosa and a base on the Chinese coast. This would cut off Japanese sea lines of communications with the resource-rich areas of Southeast Asia and enable Allied forces to blockade and strangle Japan.

While the US Navy's plan was bolder, MacArthur's strategy was more conventional and in the end more feasible. Meanwhile, events in China undermined the Nimitz–King option when a Japanese offensive (Operation *Ichi-Go*) launched in April 1944 gained ground and made it unlikely that a US base could be established in Chinese-held territory. In June 1944 MacArthur submitted a revised plan that called for an invasion of Mindanao on October 25, followed by a landing on Leyte, in the central Philippines, on November 15. This would be followed by a major landing on the main island of Luzon on January 9, 1945.

With the US Navy holding firm on a revised plan to seize Formosa, the decision on which strategy to adopt was left for President Franklin D. Roosevelt to make when he undertook an inspection tour to Hawaii in July 1944. MacArthur was at his persuasive best when he met with the Commander-in-Chief, putting forward a compelling case for his Philippines option by arguing that sound strategy and national honor demanded its implementation. Although the meeting went well for MacArthur, the details of the strategy to follow still resided with the Joint Chiefs of Staff. Their thinking was reflected in a timetable that was presented at the meeting of the Combined Chiefs of Staff in Quebec, Canada, beginning on September 11. Mindanao remained the first target, with a preferred landing date of November 15, followed by Leyte on December 20. From there, either Luzon or Formosa would be attacked.

Shortly after this timetable had been settled on, events dictated an immediate change. As the Fast Carrier Forces (designated Task Force 38) under Adm William Halsey made preparatory attacks in the Philippines, Japanese opposition seemed to crumble or was non-existent. Halsey made a recommendation to Nimitz on September 13 that the amphibious assault on Mindanao be abandoned as unnecessary, and the first landings in the Philippines be made on Leyte instead. This two-month advance in schedule was quickly approved and the invasion of Leyte set for October 20.

The US Navy assembled an overwhelming force for the assault on Leyte, with troops and their equipment being embarked in ships of the Seventh Fleet. The latter also committed a large number of escort carriers to the invasion in order to provide ground support and local air cover. Finally, a force of elderly battleships was also assembled to deal with local Japanese naval incursions.

The primary American naval force for the campaign was controlled by the Third Fleet under Halsey, and its principal operational component was TF 38. This was broken into four task groups numbered TG 38.1 through TG 38.4. Each was a powerful force in itself with four or five carriers and escorts. The total strength of TF 38 was nine fleet carriers, eight light carriers, six battleships, four heavy cruisers, ten light cruisers and some 58 destroyers. This was the world's most powerful naval force at that time, and it was capable of taking on anything the IJN could throw into battle. TF 38's orders were to support the invasion with a series of pre-landing strikes throughout the Philippines, and once the landing had been conducted, destroy any Japanese naval and air forces that threatened the landing. If the IJN fleet did make an appearance, then its destruction became Halsey's primary mission.

JAPANESE PLANS

The Americans suspected that an invasion of the Philippines would draw a Japanese response, but they did not know that the IJN had decided to make a supreme effort. Virtually every ship remaining to it was allocated a role in the defense plan, and the end result was the largest battle in naval history.

While the Americans debated their next objective after the seizure of the Marianas, the Japanese had no doubt that the Philippines would be the target. They did not know which island would be the focus of the American landing, but they were sure the Philippines were next and that the landing would occur in mid-November (which coincided with the original American plan). Accordingly, the Philippines were given top priority for preparations for the next battle, and in their defense the Japanese decided to conduct a "general decisive battle". Japan had no choice in this matter, for if the Philippines were occupied by American forces, communications with the resource-rich areas of Southeast Asia would be cut. This would in turn strangle Japan's war economy, and leave the IJN without oil for operations. Better to commit the fleet than see it waste away.

After the battle of the Philippine Sea in June 1944, the IJN's principal surface forces returned to Lingga Roads, south of Singapore, to train for the upcoming battle and, more importantly, be near to their source of fuel oil. The shattered carrier force headed back to the Japanese Home Islands, however, where the IJN set about creating new carrier air groups in the Inland Sea. If the American attack was delayed until November these carrier air groups would be ready, allowing the "flattops" to also deploy to Lingga to join the surface forces. Unfortunately for the IJN, however, the Americans were not moving to the preferred Japanese timetable. In early October the Japanese revised their intelligence estimate, stating that the American landing in the Philippines would occur on Leyte in the last ten days of the month.

The plan for the decisive battle for the defense of the Philippines was called *Sho-Go* (Victory Operation). There were several versions of the plan to deal with

Yamato and *Musashi* pictured together on October 21, 1944, in Brunei Bay. *Musashi* is to the left with heavy cruiser *Mogami* moored in front of it. To the right is *Yamato*, with another heavy cruiser alongside it. The following day, the two battleships departed Brunei Bay for Leyte Gulf. (Naval History and Heritage Command, Photo Archives, Naval Subject Collection)

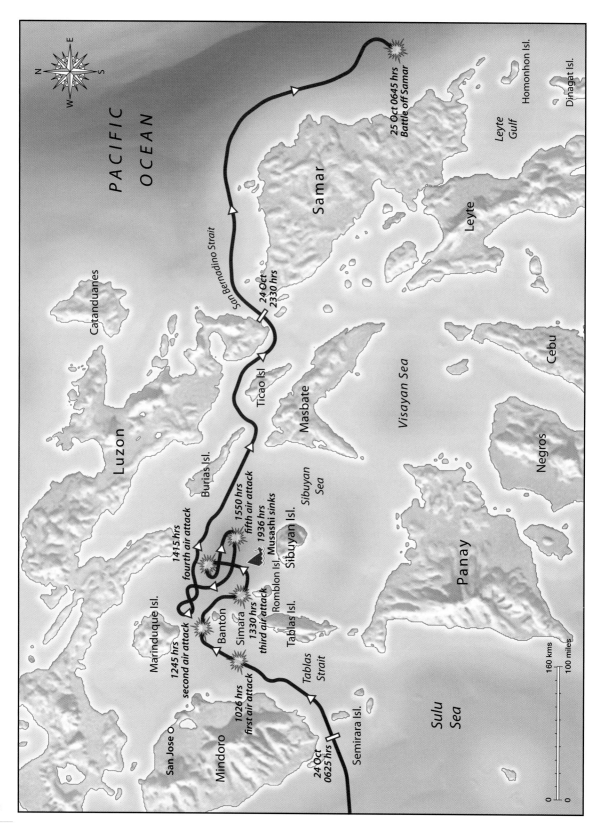

PACIFIC
OCEAN

Catanduanes Isl.

Luzon

San Bernadino Strait

24 Oct
2330 hrs

Ticao Isl.

Samar

25 Oct 0645 hrs
Battle off Samar

Homonhon Isl.

Dinagat Isl.

Leyte
Gulf

Leyte

Masbate

Burias Isl.

1550 hrs
fifth air attack

1415 hrs
fourth air attack

1936 hrs
Musashi sinks

Sibuyan
Sea

Visayan Sea

Cebu

San Jose O

Marinduque Isl.

1245 hrs
second air attack

Banton

Simara

1330 hrs
third air attack

Romblon Isl.

Sibuyan Isl.

Tablas Isl.

Negros

Mindoro

1026 hrs
first air attack

Panay

Tablas
Strait

Semirara Isl.

24 Oct
0625 hrs

Sulu
Sea

160 kms

100 miles

38

landings in the Philippines, Formosa-Ryukyus, Honshu-Kyushu and Hokkaido-Kuriles. *Sho-1* was the plan for the Philippines, and it was the one seen by the Japanese as being the most likely to be enacted. Because the IJN's carrier force was still recovering from its beating in June, and the strength of Japanese land-based air forces in the Philippines was inadequate, the success of *Sho-1* depended largely on the heavy surface forces.

The heart of the plan was to get the First Diversion Attack Force into Leyte Gulf to attack the American invasion fleet. This force, commanded by Vice Admiral Takeo Kurita, consisted of a formidable collection of warships. Available to Kurita were seven battleships (including *Yamato* and *Musashi*), 11 heavy cruisers, two light cruisers and 19 destroyers. These were divided into three sections.

The first two, with five battleships, ten heavy cruisers, two light cruisers and 15 destroyers, were under Kurita's direct command and were assigned to transit the Sibuyan Sea, pass through the San Bernardino Strait into the Philippine Sea and then enter Leyte Gulf from the north. The third section, with the two slowest battleships, a heavy cruiser and four destroyers, under Vice Admiral Shoji Nishimura, would transit the Surigao Strait and enter Leyte Gulf from the south, coincident with the movement of Kurita's force. Another smaller force, acting independently under Vice Admiral Kiyohide Shima, was designated the Second Diversion Attack Force. It too was ordered to enter Leyte Gulf through Surigao Strait. The shambolic nature of Japanese planning by this stage of the conflict meant that Shima and Nishimura failed to coordinate their operations, even though their forces would be passing through the same narrow body of water toward the same objective.

In order to make the movement of the surface forces possible, the Japanese had to find a way to neutralize or occupy Halsey's Third Fleet. The preferred method was to use land-based air power, but the parlous state of the IJN's land-based air forces in the Philippines gave this option little chance of success. All serviceable aircraft in the Philippines were to be used to attack American carriers instead, leaving no fighters available to provide air cover over Kurita's surface force. The most promising option for neutralizing Halsey's force was to use the remaining Japanese carriers, designated the Main Body and commanded by Vice Admiral Jisaburo Ozawa, to lure their US Navy equivalents to the north. This would in turn allow Kurita's force to transit unopposed though the Sibuyan Sea.

Ozawa's Main Body consisted of one fleet carrier, three light carriers, two battleships that had been converted into hybrid carriers by removing their after main gun turrets and replacing them with a short flightdeck, three light cruisers and eight destroyers. This was a toothless force since the ships carried just 116 aircraft between them – a total approximately equal to the strength of a carrier air group embarked in a single American fleet carrier. Nevertheless, Ozawa's force was tasked with playing a key role in *Sho-1*, as the survival of Kurita's First Diversion Attack Force hinged on the Main Body successfully engaging TF 38.

The plan had significant weaknesses. The first was the underlying premise that surface forces could operate without air cover and move significant distances under enemy air attack and still achieve their objectives. Another important

Track of the First Diversion Attack Force on 24–25 October 1944. The heart of the IJN's plan to repel the American invasion of Leyte was the powerful First Diversion Attack Force, which included both *Yamato* and *Musashi*. To get to Leyte Gulf, this force would have to transit the Sibuyan Sea and then exit through the San Bernardino Strait, all probably under American attack. In fact the passage through the Sibuyan Sea brought a total of five waves of attacking US Navy carrier aircraft. These focused on *Musashi*, which was crippled by an intense torpedo- and dive-bombing attack and sank that evening. Its wreck was discovered in March 2015 in water 1,120ft deep by a private exploration team funded by American billionaire, and Microsoft co-founder, Paul Allen. The remainder of the First Diversion Attack Force suffered only light damage, however, and just before midnight transited the San Bernardino Strait unmolested. The following day, *Yamato* would use its 18.1in. guns against American ships for the only time during the war in the battle off Samar.

tuition focused on the skills required for each type of aircraft and trained the pilot to land on aircraft carriers. At the conclusion of operational training, the new naval aviator possessed about 350 hours of flying time.

The real preparation for combat began when the new pilot was assigned to a squadron as part of a carrier air group that was preparing to deploy to the Pacific. Here, the pilot learned the tactics and skills for actual combat. The time taken to work up a carrier air group was considerable, even on top of the almost one year of training that the new pilot brought with him. For example, Carrier Air Group 18 was established on July 20, 1943, under the command of combat veteran Cdr William Ellis. The three squadrons assigned to the carrier air group began as rivals, but the constant training had eventually turned them into a well-meshed team when, on February 24, 1944, they finally departed California for Hawaii. The three squadrons continued to train extensively once in the central Pacific, but they had problems executing joint operations that were essential if the coordinated attack tactics against ships were to be conducted effectively. In July, Carrier Air Group 18 finally deployed aboard the Essex-class carrier USS *Intrepid* (CV-11) and almost immediately went into action.

By 1945, the US Navy was feeling the need for fresh naval aviators. The decision to reduce the number of pilots it was sending through the training pipeline the previous year in anticipation of the war's end was now proving to be an embarrassing mistake, and it had had to be reversed. Despite this hiccup, the quality of naval aviation training remained high. Carrier air groups were commanded by combat veterans and new pilots seeing combat for the first time averaged 525 hours of accumulated flying time.

Officers of VT-6 pose in front of their Avengers in February 1944. The squadron was embarked aboard *Intrepid* from January to March 1944 when Carrier Air Group 6 replaced Carrier Air Group 18 after the latter had had problems executing joint operations that were essential if the coordinated attack tactics against ships were to be conducted effectively. Although losses suffered by Avenger and Helldiver squadrons in individual attacks on IJN ships were usually low, the cumulative attrition from constant combat and operational mishaps was heavy, which necessitated a continual rotation of squadrons on frontline carriers. (Real War Photos)

TBM AVENGER COCKPIT

1. Gunsight
2. Manifold pressure gauge
3. Altimeter
4. Airspeed indicator
5. Ammunition rounds counter
6. Ammunition rounds counter
7. Ammunition rounds counter
8. Tachometer
9. Rate of climb indicator
10. Turn and bank indicator
11. Compass
12. Attitude gyro
13. AYD altitude control
14. Oil temperature gauge
15. Cockpit light (x2)
16. Pull-out chart board
17. Radio altitude indicator
18. Fuel hand pump
19. Ignition switch
20. Cowl flaps control
21. Bomb-bay doors control
22. Chart board light
23. Wing lock safety control handle
24. Engine triple gauge unit
25. Fuel quantity gauges

26. ARB receiver remote tuner
27. Oil intercooler shutters control
28. Throttle control
29. Supercharger control
30. Cylinder head temperature gauge
31. Landing gear control handle
32. Landing flaps control
33. Rudder pedals
34. Oil pressure gauge
35. Gun charging controls
36. Fuel pressure gauge

37. Check list plate
38. Elevator trim tab control
39. Rudder trim tab control
40. Elevator trim wheel
41. Suction gauge
42. Pilot's seat
43. Manual reset circuit breaker panel
44. Main electrical distribution panel
45. AN/ARC-5 pilot's receiver control unit
46. ARB receiver control unit
47. Recognition lights control unit
48. Main armament panel
49. ADF automatic direction finder
50. Fuel selector valve
51. Armament switches
52. Control column grip
53. Propeller control
54. Landing gear and wing flap position indicator
55. Hydraulic hand pump
56. AYD indicator lights
57. Pilot's armrest

However, by late 1944, there were signs of stress in fleet units, with many carrier air groups finding it difficult to finish their prescribed six-month combat tours because of the very high tempo of operations in the Pacific. This, combined with the increased kamikaze threat, quickly caused combat fatigue and required that emergency replacements be fed into the squadrons whilst they were still embarked. Nevertheless, the naval aviators that took on *Yamato* and *Musashi* were the finest in the world.

US NAVY SHIP ATTACK TACTICS

By 1944, US Navy carrier air groups had a well-rehearsed and proven doctrine for attacking Japanese naval targets. The key was to launch a coordinated strike with fighters and dive- and torpedo-bombers in order to overwhelm the target's defenses. Earlier in the war, this proved consistently difficult for American carrier air groups to achieve, but by 1944 communications and doctrinal difficulties had been overcome to allow this to occur on a routine basis. Each carrier air group conducted its own attack, although by 1944 an overall attack coordinator was usually present to direct aircraft to the best target and avoid over- or under-concentration on a single target.

The actual attack tactic was simple. The Hellcats preceded the strike in order to engage any Japanese fighters over the objective. Once the way was clear, the Helldivers would attack first. The standard dive-bombing profile was to begin in a shallow approach from 20,000ft and enter into a steep dive between 15,000ft and 12,000ft. The 18-aircraft Helldiver squadron was divided into three divisions, each with six aircraft, which would overwhelm the target by approaching from different directions. Ideally, a ship was attacked along its longitudinal axis. This presented as large a target as possible, and explained why Japanese ships typically used a circular evasion maneuver to give the dive-bomber pilots a constantly changing target axis. The dive was typically made at an angle of 65–70 degrees, with the 1,000lb bomb being dropped 1,500–2,000ft above the target.

An Avenger pilot from VT-16 goes to full power prior to commencing his takeoff roll from USS *Lexington* (CV-16) on November 28, 1943. The TBF is loaded with 250lb bombs, VT-16 supporting VB-16 and VF-16 in an attack on the Marshall Islands. Besides being able to carry the Mark 13 torpedo, the Avenger could carry up to 2,000lb of bombs, which made it a mainstay for ground attack missions. (Naval History and Heritage Command, Photo Archives, Naval Subject Collection)

Helldivers from VB-7, embarked in USS *Hancock* (CV-19), strafe Japanese shipping in Manila harbor on November 25, 1944. Although this was not the typical attack profile for a Helldiver, the aircraft's two wing-mounted 20mm cannon could devastate smaller ships such as these. (Real War Photos)

After clearing away any enemy Zero-sens that were present, the fighters had a role in the attack phase as well. They dove from their patrol altitude of 10,000ft and strafed the ship being attacked to reduce the target's air defenses and divert attention from the torpedo-bombers.

The key to an attack on a heavily armored ship such as *Yamato* or *Musashi* was the last part of the combined strike – the torpedo attack. By 1945, the US Navy had refined its torpedo attack tactics in the face of trial and error in combat. The attacks made early in the war, which came in low and slow, had given way to new tactics that emphasized a high and fast delivery. This greatly increased the survivability of the aircraft conducting the attack. Tests had indicated that the best profile for an attack was at 260 knots from a height of 800ft. This increased the chances that the Mark 13 would work as advertised. With this profile, the US Navy expected that 92 percent of torpedoes would function properly.

The preferred attack was called an "anvil" attack that called for Avengers to simultaneously approach the target from either side of the bow, making it all but impossible for the target to maneuver without exposing itself to attack. For Avenger pilots, getting the right launch profile took good

Early-production TBFs conduct torpedo attack training – sorties such as this one were regularly flown in an effort to keep the pilots' skills honed in this difficult tactic. The leading Avengers have already broken away following their drops, and the next aircraft in line has released its torpedo. Depending on the estimated speed and range of the target ship, wingmen would add or subtract five-knot increments to their torpedo drop times in an attempt to bracket their target with a "comb" of weapons that would ensure at least one hit from either beam. Properly executed, a squadron-sized attack could be completed in less than one minute from the run-in point to drop. Barely 20 seconds later, one or more torpedoes should strike the target. If this scene depicted actual combat, the Avengers would be more widely separated. (Naval History and Heritage Command, Photo Archives, Naval Subject Collection)

airmanship and constant practice. The pilot had to judge his speed, altitude and glide angle and then launch the weapon the correct distance from the target. The glide angle was key – the torpedo needed to be released in a shallow dive for maximum reliability. If the angle was too steep, the torpedo could be damaged upon water entry, and if the angle was too slow, the weapon's controls might not work properly. If these were all correct and the Avenger came in at 260 knots and 800ft, this meant that the torpedo

ENGAGING THE ENEMY

The pilot of an Avenger had to be both brave and skilled to be an effective torpedo-bomber. This cockpit view shows the ideal set-up for a torpedo attack. The pilot had to simultaneously take into account multiple factors in order to make the right approach, including his speed, altitude, glide angle and the correct launch distance from the target. The Mark 13 torpedo had to be treated with care. If the glide angle was too steep, the torpedo could be damaged upon entering the water. If the angle was too shallow, the torpedo controls might malfunction.

If the pilot was skillful enough to assess all these factors correctly, the Avenger would approach the target at 260 knots and at an altitude of 800ft. At this speed and altitude, the torpedo would fall for seven

seconds at an angle of 28 degrees while covering 3,000ft between the time the weapon was dropped and when it entered the water. To ensure that the Mark 13 had time to arm, it had to run for 1,200ft to the target. All of this data when combined meant that the correct distance for a drop was 4,200ft (1,400 yards) from where the pilot judged the target would be.

In this view, an Avenger is approaching the starboard side of *Yamato* as the ship steams at high speed and desperately throws up a barrage of 5in. and 25mm fire. At this point in his run, the pilot must keep a steady course to the target to ensure a precise drop. Once the torpedo is away, he will dive for the deck and exit the area as quickly as possible.

would fall for seven seconds at an angle of 28 degrees while covering 3,000ft between the time the weapon was dropped and when it entered the water.

To make sure the weapon armed, the torpedo had to run for 1,200ft before hitting the target. Dropping at this distance also minimized the time the target had for evasive maneuvers. This meant that the correct distance for a drop was 4,200ft (1,400 yards) from where the pilot judged the target would be.

Judging the range to the target also took skill, with naval aviators often underestimating how far away the ship was. In order to prevent such mistakes from occurring, the crew was helped by the radar fitted to the Avenger, which could give a range to the target as the aircraft approached. If the torpedo was launched too early, the target had a greater opportunity to evade. If it was released too late, the torpedo would not arm. A trained eye could also determine when to launch against a ship conducting evasive maneuvers, since practice gave the pilot an understanding of how quickly a ship could turn and how much speed it lost when doing so.

During an actual attack run, this maneuver usually had to be executed whilst the Avenger came under enemy fire. To throw the aim of the Japanese gunners off, the pilot would weave his TBM from side to side and occasionally change altitude. However, the aircraft had to be stable in the moments preceding the torpedo drop. Once the weapon had departed the aircraft, the Avenger would bank and hug the deck until it was out of range of the Japanese guns. Despite the development of these tactics, US Navy torpedo-bombers were still handicapped by their faulty weapons early in the war.

The first instance of a torpedo attack in combat was on March 10, 1942, when VT-2's TBDs, embarked in USS *Lexington* (CV-2), engaged a Japanese invasion force bound for New Guinea off Lae and Salamaua. The attack caught the Japanese by surprise, so the targets had no air cover and were moving at low speed. Even so, only a single transport was sunk by the 13 torpedoes launched. On May 4, VT-5's TBDs, flying from USS *Yorktown* (CV-5), attacked Japanese ships at anchor off Tulagi and nearby islands. This time, of 22 torpedoes launched in two attacks, only one hit. The high point of the Mark 13's early war career was recorded three days later when 22 TBDs engaged the light carrier *Shoho*. The first wave of 12 TBDs from VT-2 had time

The finest moment of the Devastator and the Mark 13 torpedo came on May 7, 1942, when two squadrons attacked the Japanese light carrier *Shoho*. Here, a USS *Lexington* (CV-2) TBD from VT-2 can be seen dropping its torpedo (note the splash) and turning away. Under perfect conditions and with a variant of the Mark 13 less prone to malfunction, a large number of hits were scored. (Naval History and Heritage Command)

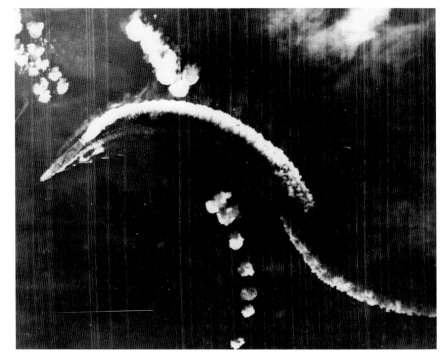

This well-known photo of the IJN carrier *Hiryu* during the Battle of Midway amply demonstrates the difficulty of hitting maneuvering targets at sea from high altitude. Here, *Hiryu* avoids several salvos of 500lb bombs dropped from B-17s flying at 20,000ft. The ineffectiveness of high-altitude bombing forced both the IJN and US Navy to rely on dive-bombers. (Naval History and Heritage Command)

The US Navy's first experience with attacking Japanese battleships with aircraft occurred on November 13, 1942. *Hiei* had been damaged in a surface action the previous night, incurring damage to its steering gear that left the ship unable to leave the area. The following day it was subjected to more than 70 sorties, which inflicted further damage. However, the ship was in no danger of sinking until four torpedo hits were scored by Avengers. (Naval History and Heritage Command, Photo Archives, Naval Subject Collection)

to set up an anvil attack on the light carrier thanks to minimal antiaircraft fire and no fighter opposition. Nine hits were claimed and five were confirmed, the torpedo-bombers having the advantage of attacking a target that was already dead in the water following a previous dive-bomber attack. When the ten TBDs from *Yorktown* arrived, they all lined up to attack the carrier's starboard side and scored several hits from close range.

The events of May 7 demonstrated that the Mark 13 torpedo could work if the TBDs conducted a slow-speed run (less than 110 knots) at low altitude. This was not possible if the target had any kind of defense, however. Also, VT-2's torpedoes were older but more reliable Mod 0 weapons.

The next day, the Devastator–Mark 13 combination showed its limitations in a more contested environment. This time the target was the fast and well-defended fleet carrier *Shokaku*. *Yorktown*'s well-trained carrier air group executed a coordinated attack, with the TBDs coming in just as the dive-bombers attacked – nine Devastators launched their weapons from 1,000–2,000 yards and none of the torpedoes hit home, with several being seen to run erratically. The 11 TBDs from *Lexington* that targeted the carrier fared even worse, since *Shokaku* was actually able to outrun the torpedoes!

The debacle at the battle of the Coral Sea was followed by an even greater disaster that brought the

TBD's combat career to a bloody end. Of 41 TBDs committed by three squadrons to attack the Japanese carrier force at the Battle of Midway in June 1942, only 11 were able to launch their weapons – which were easily avoided – and just six survived the heavy fighter opposition.

The Avenger experienced no success with torpedoes during the two carrier battles of the Guadalcanal campaign. However, on November 13, 1942, it showed that under ideal conditions effective torpedo attacks could be delivered. The previous night, the IJN battleship *Hiei* had been damaged in a surface engagement and left unmaneuverable because of damage to its steering compartment. The Americans flew 70 sorties throughout the day to finish the ship off, and amongst the aircraft involved were Avengers armed with the Mark 13 torpedo. Despite being one of the IJN's oldest battleships, and possessing little in the way of air cover or maneuverability, *Hiei* proved difficult to sink. The Avengers scored two torpedo hits early in the day, but the ship was in no danger of sinking. In the afternoon, two additional torpedo hits ended any hope of salvage by the Japanese.

In the next major fleet engagement – the battle of the Philippine Sea – in June 1944, most Avengers were carrying bombs instead of torpedoes since frontline units had neglected torpedo tactics since late 1942. However, there was a noteworthy success on June 20 when Avengers from VT-24, embarked in the light carrier USS *Belleau Wood* (CVL-24), put a torpedo into the light carrier *Hiyo* and sank it. In contrast, the three IJN carriers hit by bombs all survived.

IJN WARSHIP CREWS

The IJN was famous for the rigor of its fleet training and exercise program. This was another essential element of the IJN's plans to compensate for its numerical weakness relative to the US Navy. This strategy of a small, intensively trained force could not survive the requirements of war, however, when the IJN reluctantly lowered its standards in order to expand the fleet and replace losses. Nevertheless, *Yamato* and *Musashi* were presumably manned by handpicked sailors since they were the pride of the fleet. Japanese warship crews typically experienced little turnover, so the prewar cadre of the crew of *Yamato* remained largely intact, as did the early war crew of *Musashi*. Both crews were proud to serve on such powerful warships and longed to finally get into action.

Even with the war clearly going against Japan by 1944, the crews of *Yamato* and *Musashi* had maintained their high morale. Both looked forward to being employed in an operation where they could show what their ships were capable of. Although conditions on board the super battleships were becoming cramped by then, they were still luxurious by IJN standards. Each member of the crew had more personal space than on any other Japanese warship, which made living accommodations on the two battleships the best in the IJN. Officers had their own staterooms and petty officers had separate quarters from the junior enlisted personnel.

During the war, the crews of both ships were expanded. The primary reason for this was the proliferation of antiaircraft guns – each 25mm triple mount took nine men

FLEET ADMIRAL WILLIAM F. HALSEY

William F. Halsey was one of the pioneers of naval aviation in the US Navy and the author of the destruction of *Musashi*. After graduation from the US Naval Academy in 1904, Halsey spent most of his early career on torpedo boats and destroyers. His career took a radical change of course when, in 1934, the then Chief of the Bureau of Aeronautics, Ernest King, offered him command of the carrier USS *Saratoga* (CV-3). However, by law, carrier commanders had to be naval aviators, which meant that Halsey would first have to finish a 12-week aviation course for senior commanders prior to taking charge of the ship. He earned his aviator's wings on May 15, 1935, at the age of 52, making him the oldest aviator in the fleet.

Halsey was promoted to rear admiral in 1938, and by the start of the Pacific War in December 1941 he was both the senior carrier division commander in the US Navy and Commander, Aircraft Battle Force. Halsey was firmly convinced that aviation would be the US Navy's primary offensive weapon, and the Japanese raid on Pearl Harbor made his case for him. Now the US Navy's handful of carriers became the centerpiece of the Pacific Fleet. Adm Chester W. Nimitz, Commander-in-Chief, US Pacific Fleet, used them to raid Japanese-held islands. By far the most aggressive carrier commander in the early months of the campaign in 1942 was Halsey. He and his beloved flagship USS *Enterprise* (CV-6) participated in raids against the Gilberts and Marshalls in February, Wake Island in March and, finally, in the most daring of them all, the Doolittle Raid, mounted against the Japanese Home Islands in April.

A skin condition caused Halsey to miss Midway, but as soon as he was fit for duty he was sent by Nimitz to Guadalcanal to pump energy into the faltering American offensive. This proved to be Halsey's finest moment. While the IJN refused to commit all of its resources, including the battleship *Yamato*, which sat idle at Truk, Halsey threw whatever he had at his disposal into the fight to repel major Japanese offensives in

October and November. On several occasions he was reckless, committing both of his carriers beyond the range of land-based air support at the battle of Santa Cruz and then two modern battleships in the torpedo-infested waters off Guadalcanal at night, but both times fortune favored the bold, and Halsey was applauded for his aggressiveness.

During 1943, Halsey fought his way up the Solomons to eventually isolate the major Japanese base at Rabaul. A key moment of this campaign came in November of that year when a daring air attack by two of Halsey's carrier air groups crippled a large force of Japanese heavy cruisers in Rabaul. This risky operation saved the American beachhead on Bougainville Island from attack.

In May 1944, Halsey was given command of the Third Fleet. He continued with his trademark aggressiveness and led the Fast Carrier Task Force in a series of raids to prepare for the invasion of the Philippines. This led to Halsey's most controversial decision of the war when, during the battle for Leyte Gulf, he ordered the Third Fleet north to attack the toothless Japanese carriers after battering the First Diversion Attack Force. In so doing, he left the San Bernardino Strait unguarded, thus allowing Kurita's force to head south to attack the Seventh Fleet's vastly inferior escort carrier force. Halsey stated that he did this so as not to divide his forces, but in reality his overwhelming strength would have allowed him to have split his Fast Carrier Task Force and still enjoyed superiority over the

enemy. In fact, on October 25, he divided his force several times in response to the cries from the Seventh Fleet for help.

Halsey did finally send his fastest battleships in an effort to prevent Kurita from returning by the San Bernardino Strait, but he missed the Japanese fleet by just a few hours. His actions allowed Kurita's force to escape, thus denying *Yamato* a chance to engage American battleships.

TYPE 96 25mm AA GUNS

This artwork depicts a Type 96 25mm triple antiaircraft gun mount on *Yamato* engaging Avenger torpedo-bombers of VT-84 on April 7, 1945. A crew of nine was required to service the weapon – six of these were loaders to keep the three guns fed with 15-round magazine clips. The scene shows the loaders working furiously to remove the clips from the ready ammunition storage lockers located around the gun position so as to keep up the mount's rate of fire.

The Type 96 had a number of shortcomings that ultimately made it ineffective as the IJN's primary short-range antiaircraft weapon. Among these was the requirement to frequently change the ammunition clips, which reduced the actual rate of fire to 100–110 rounds per minute. In addition, the 25mm shells weighed under 9 ounces, which often meant they caused little damage even if they hit the rugged Avenger. The 25mm gun was limited to close-in engagements only. By doctrine this meant opening fire at approaching aircraft at about 2,750 yards.

Fire control for the Type 96 was provided by Type 95 or Type 4 directors, but these were largely ineffective in tracking fast targets. As an alternative, the mount could be fired under local control. To aid in this, every fifth round was a tracer, so the crew could track its fire relative to the target.

Despite its shortcomings, the Type 96 was the most effective IJN antiaircraft weapon. However, it needs to be kept in mind that the overall ineffectiveness of the Type 96 exposed Japanese surface ships to crippling air attack. This in turn meant that only 18 US Navy aircraft were lost throughout October 24, 1944 while attacking the First Diversion Attack Force, and that the entire *Yamato* force only downed ten aircraft on April 7, 1945.

A VB-13 pilot examines flak damage to his aircraft aboard USS *Franklin* (CV-13) after attacking *Musashi* on October 24, 1944. In the background, his gunner can be seen carrying both parachutes on the starboard wing of the Helldiver. VB-13 flew from "Big Ben" between July and October 1944. (Peter Mersky)

to operate it, in addition to the personnel required to man the fire control equipment, move ammunition from magazines and to provide basic support for the gunners. Conditions on *Yamato* were so crowded by 1945 that personnel had to sleep in hammocks in passageways or in any other available space.

The crew of *Musashi* underwent a particularly rigorous preparation program whilst under the command of Capt Toshihira Inoguchi. His background was in gunnery, and his reputation as one of the best gunnery officers in the IJN led him to be given the responsibility of commanding one of the two most powerful battleships in the world. With plenty of fuel available at Lingga, Inoguchi conducted extensive at-sea training.

Having studied the *Sho-Go* plan, he understood that his ship would be subjected to extensive air attack, and it had to survive this to accomplish the mission. He trained his antiaircraft crews relentlessly and devised a layered defense to protect his ship, with the 18in. guns for long-range defense, the 5in. guns at intermediate range, and the numerous 25mm mounts for short-range defense.

Inoguchi was not naive, and he assumed a ship operating without air cover under the threat of severe air attack would be damaged. The ship's damage control personnel had to be ready, therefore. He trained these crews extensively, damage control engineers exercising the ship's counter-flooding procedures to correct lists created by Inoguchi. Twice daily, the entire crew had to make the ship watertight. It was no easy task to set the maximum watertight condition on an IJN ship, since the latches on doors and hatches were not quick acting. Constant drill was required to achieve a watertight condition in the shortest time possible. In addition, the ship trained for offensive tactics, practicing to break into an anchorage filled with American shipping. As events would prove, the crew were as combat ready as they could be, and the damage-control personnel soon proved their proficiency.

JAPANESE ANTIAIRCRAFT TACTICS

The IJN viewed fighters as the primary means of defending surface ships against American air attack. This worked fairly well early in the war, but depended on high-quality pilots. By October 1944 these did not exist, and the effectiveness of the IJN's carrier force had been reduced to such an extent that it was being used as a decoy only. This meant the surface fleet was on its own against American air power.

To contend with this growing threat, the IJN placed more and more antiaircraft guns on fleet units. Most of these were 25mm guns that could be located almost anywhere with a clear arc of fire. Destroyers carried up to 26 25mm guns, heavy cruisers up to 60 and battleships more than 100. As previously mentioned, *Yamato* and *Musashi* eventually boasted 152 and 130, respectively.

Even with the augmentation of ships' antiaircraft suites, the IJN did not think that such weapons alone would protect its surface fleet from air attack. This was indicated by how vigorously Japanese ships maneuvered when under aerial attack. Instead of maintaining formation and keeping a steady course, which would allow the massing of antiaircraft fire and the best possible fire solution, IJN ships radically maneuvered independently of one another in an effort to reduce their chances of being hit. A circular evasive maneuver was often observed by American pilots, although IJN doctrine called for zigzag-like maneuvering. This not only made it difficult for the pilot of a dive-bomber to pick an aim point, it also made a torpedo-bomber pilot's job more

A damaged Helldiver from VB-15 prepares to land on board *Essex* despite a large section of its vertical stabilizer having been shot away by IJN flak. Between May and November 1944, "Bombing 15" attacked Japanese bases and shipping in the Marianas, Palaus, Formosa, Okinawa and the Philippines, dueling with IJN gunners on numerous occasions. The squadron was credited with sinking or damaging a record tonnage of Japanese merchant and naval ships. (Naval History and Heritage Command, Photo Archives, Naval Subject Collection)

VICE ADMIRAL TAKEO KURITA

Takeo Kurita was the single most important Japanese commander in the entire *Sho-1* scheme. He had been promoted to flag rank in November 1938, and by the start of the Pacific War he was in command of Sentai 7, which was comprised of the four Mogami-class heavy cruisers. In this capacity, Kurita saw considerable action in the early stages of the conflict.

His cruisers supported the invasion of Java in 1942, where he finished off the heavy cruiser USS *Houston* (CA-30). This was followed by a raid into the Indian Ocean that saw Kurita's cruisers play the lead role in sinking 135,000 tons of Allied shipping in the Bay of Bengal. However, in June he had an early taste of US Navy air power when carrier aircraft sank one of his cruisers and heavily damaged another at the Battle of Midway. In July, Kurita was assigned as commander of Sentai 3, overseeing the operations of two Kongo-class battleships. Under his command, *Kongo* and *Haruna* conducted a devastating bombardment of Henderson Field, on Guadalcanal, during the night of October 13, their barrage temporarily neutralizing the airfield. It was the most successful action undertaken by the IJN's battleships during the entire war.

In 1943 Kurita was named commander of the Second Fleet, which was the formation containing most of the IJN's battleships and heavy cruisers. He led it during the battle of the Philippine Sea, where he supported the carriers. Kurita and his ships would have a central role in the defense of the Philippines, since he was in command of the First Diversion Attack Force. It had the seemingly impossible task of breaking into Leyte Gulf.

Many officers in his force were appalled that the fleet was being risked to attack mere transports, and they doubted that they would ever get close to Leyte Gulf. Kurita discussed the details of *Sho-1* with his subordinates on October 21. He probably had his own concerns about the plan, but after many of those present had the opportunity to express their doubts, Kurita reminded them of the "glorious opportunity" they had been given. He called on his men to make the ultimate sacrifice, asking them "Would it not be a shame to have the fleet remain intact while the nation perishes?" Kurita finished his rousing briefing with the following question. "What man can say that there is no chance for our fleet to turn the tide of war in a decisive battle?"

Whatever his pre-battle rhetoric, Kurita's behavior during the engagement itself suggests that he did not subscribe to the do-or-die mission he was being asked to perform. At the fateful moment when he could have made a dash for Leyte Gulf and reached the objective given to him, thus gaining some measure of a Pyrrhic victory for the IJN, he declined the opportunity. No doubt he realized that once in Leyte Gulf, his chances of getting out again were minimal.

After seeing *Musashi* pounded under the waves on October 24, Kurita temporarily turned back to the west so as to allow Japanese air power to attack Halsey's carriers, thus lessening the weight of attack on his unprotected surface ships. After being ordered by Adm Soemu Toyoda (Commander-in-Chief of the Combined Fleet) to resume course to San Bernardino Strait, he transited the strait without opposition and headed south along Samar towards Leyte Gulf. On the morning of October 25, Kurita received the miracle he had hoped for when he surprised a force of American carriers. He almost immediately lost control of the action, however, and never brought his advantage to bear. He remained unaware throughout the engagement that he was fighting a group of slow, unarmored light carriers with a weak escort. After sinking one escort carrier and three escorts, Kurita broke off the action. This was the only occasion in the war when *Yamato* fired on an American surface target.

After the engagement with the escort carriers, Kurita ordered his force to regroup to the north, away from his objective of Leyte Gulf. By this time the news of Vice Admiral Nishimura's defeat at Surigao Strait and of the destruction of Vice Admiral Ozawa's carriers was coming in. After contemplating his options, Kurita broke off the operation and headed back through San Bernardino Strait. The supreme sacrifices of the IJN during the battle to permit Kurita's force to reach Leyte Gulf had been in vain. Kurita's action did save the bulk of his fleet and *Yamato*, but his failure to press the attack meant the failure of the entire *Sho-1* operation. He was criticized for this failure and was removed from command in December. Well after the war he admitted that he withdrew his fleet because he did not want to waste the lives of his men in a futile operation, proving that courage can indeed take several forms.

challenging. The downside was that this kind of radical maneuvering ruined attempts at gaining a fire-control solution on either enemy aircraft or surface ships. It also broke up a formation so that ships could no longer provide mutually protecting fire.

Maneuvering a ship as large as *Yamato* was challenging. This is how a surviving officer described the super battleship's attempts at avoiding torpedo attacks in April 1945:

> The tracks of torpedoes are a beautiful white against the water. Estimating by sight their distance and angle on the plotting board, we shift course to run parallel to the torpedoes and barely succeed in dodging them. We deal first with the closest, most urgent, one. When we get to a point far enough away from it that we can be sure we have dodged it, we turn to the next. Dealing with them calls for vigilance, calculation and decision. The captain is out in the open in the anti-aircraft command post overlooking the whole ship. Two ensigns attend him and plot on a maneuver board the torpedoes coming from all directions, indicating to him with pointers.

The basis for antiaircraft action against US Navy dive-bombers and low-flying torpedo-bombers was barrage fire. Only against more predictable high-level bombers was aimed fire envisioned. Barrage fire was used by crews manning both medium-caliber 5in. weapons and 25mm short-range guns. The 5in. guns would be used primarily against level bombers at medium altitude and dive-bombers, while the 25mm guns targeted both dive-bombers and, when required, torpedo-bombers. The 5in. guns would, on occasion, also target torpedo-bombers, initially opening fire when the aircraft were at a distance of about 7,500 yards. Dive-bombers were engaged by 5in. guns at an altitude of about 10,000ft. A captured Japanese wartime document indicated that the 25mm battery was to open fire at 2,750 yards. Gunners were to conserve ammunition since stocks on board were finite, and rounds had to be conserved to deal with sustained attacks. Retreating targets were not to be engaged.

The Japanese knew that their antiaircraft defenses were inadequate to address the increasing scale of American air attacks. The difficulty of hitting targets was summed up by a survivor from *Yamato*:

> In aiming torpedoes and bombs, one must hold to a given course for a certain distance. But the American aircraft reduce that vulnerability to the very minimum. Targets that attack even while we are zigzagging from left to right necessitate sizable and swift corrections in aim both horizontally and vertically. Aiming at such a target is far too difficult for simple machine guns. Our percentage of hits is, therefore, very low.
>
> For each five rounds, the guns fire one tracer shell. By watching how the tracer's tea-colored trajectory intersects the target, the gunners ascertain their error and adjust for distance and angle. Still, when the angular velocity is so great, a hit is difficult, even at very close range.

The US Navy assessed in mid-1944 that the Japanese were using barrage fire for antiaircraft defense. The 25mm gun was judged to be the most effective weapon, having caused three times the number of casualties as the 5in. gun.

COMBAT

TREK OF THE FIRST DIVERSION ATTACK FORCE

On the morning of October 17, Japanese observers on Suluan Island, in the eastern approaches to Leyte Gulf, reported the approach of US Navy ships. This was enough to confirm the Japanese suspicion that Leyte was the target of the American invasion. Accordingly, the Commander-in-Chief of the Combined Fleet, Adm Soemu Toyoda, ordered that all forces for *Sho-1* go on alert. When he was absolutely sure of American intentions, Toyoda ordered the execution of *Sho-1* at 1110hrs on October 18. The date for the IJN to enter Leyte Gulf and crush the American landing force was set for the morning of October 25.

As the Japanese made their preparations, the main American landing on Leyte occurred on October 20 against weak opposition. The initial assault ships were quickly unloaded and had departed by evening. Several reinforcement echelons followed, and by October 25, 132,400 men and just under 200,000 tons of supplies were ashore through the two main landing areas. This showed the futility of the *Sho-1* plan, since it was seeking to dislodge a landing force already firmly ashore and ready for sustained operations. The only shipping in Leyte Gulf by midnight on October 24 were three flagships, one assault transport, 23 tank landing ships, two medium landing ships and 28 Liberty ships. Even if the IJN had successfully entered Leyte Gulf and sunk every one of these ships, it would not have translated into an appreciable delay in American operations.

The First Diversion Attack Force departed from Lingga at 0100hrs on October 18 and headed to Brunei Bay on the north coast of Borneo. Here, the ships refueled and Vice Admiral Kurita took the opportunity to confer with his officers. At 0800hrs on October 22, Kurita's force departed Brunei and headed northeast through the Palawan Passage. Nishimura's force departed at 1500hrs later that same day and headed through the Balabac Strait into the Sulu Sea.

Although he was out of range of American aircraft, Kurita had not gone far before he encountered trouble. The submarines USS *Dace* (SS-247) and USS *Darter* (SS-227) were operating off the southern entrance of the Palawan Passage. *Darter* picked up the approaching Japanese ships on radar at 0116hrs on October 23, its skipper duly sending a contact report and then heading off to engage them. Kurita was aware that American submarines were in the area, but inexplicably he failed to send any destroyers ahead of his force, which was arranged in two sections.

In a perfect ambush, *Darter* attacked Kurita's flagship, the heavy cruiser *Atago*, with its bow torpedo tubes and then swung around to fire its stern tubes at the next ship in the column, the heavy cruiser *Takao*. Meanwhile, *Dace* fired a full salvo at the heavy cruiser *Maya*. At this range the results were devastating. *Atago* and *Maya* were sunk, and two hits on *Takao* forced the ship to return to Brunei. Kurita survived *Atago*'s sinking, but he had to swim for his life before being rescued by a destroyer and transferred to *Yamato* to resume command. As if the attack itself had not been devastating enough, the Americans now knew the location of Kurita's force.

Musashi is seen at 0900hrs on October 22 after leaving Brunei Bay. The Aichi E13A Type 0 "Jake" reconnaissance seaplanes on the stern were flown off before the ship came under air attack two days later. (Naval History and Heritage Command, Photo Archives, Naval Subject Collection)

US NAVY RESPONDS

Halsey doubted whether the IJN would make a major attempt to disrupt the invasion of Leyte, but by October 23 it was clear that the Japanese were in fact doing just that – even though Ozawa's Main Body had not yet been sighted. The emergence of the IJN wrong-footed Halsey, since his strongest task group, TG 38.1, was well south of the battle area on its way to the base at Ulithi to replenish. He ordered his other three task groups to close on the Philippine coast to be ready to launch search aircraft and strikes from the 24th.

The light aircraft carrier USS *Cabot* (CVL-28) was assigned with *Intrepid* to TG 38.2 during the battle of Leyte Gulf, and the former's Carrier Air Group 29 was very active during the attacks on *Musashi* on October 25. Here, *Cabot* is shown maneuvering under Japanese kamikaze attack on November 25 – the same day that *Intrepid* was struck by two kamikazes. (Real War Photos)

Following the debacle in the Palawan Passage, Kurita continued to track to the northeast and soon entered the Mindoro Strait. Here, an American submarine spotted the force after midnight on October 24, but it was unable to get into a position to attack. Later that morning the IJN fleet was spotted by one of TG 38.2's morning search aircraft at 0810hrs off Semirara Island, to the south of Mindoro. Minutes later the contact report reached the commander of TG 38.2, and preparations were made to launch an immediate attack.

When it came to engaging the First Diversion Attack Force on October 24, TG 38.2 was on its own for much of the day. TG 38.3 was too far north to launch immediate strikes and TG 38.4 was too far south. TG 38.2 was the weakest of TF 38's four task groups, with fleet carrier *Intrepid* and light carriers USS *Cabot* (CVL-28) and *Independence* (CVL-22). The carrier air group embarked in CVL-22 was dedicated to night operations, so its aircraft played no part in the attacks on Kurita's force.

TG 38.2's first strike was comprised of 45 aircraft – 21 Hellcats, 12 Helldivers and 12 Avengers. Of these, ten Hellcats (VF-29) and four Avengers (VT-29) came from *Cabot*, with the remainder from *Intrepid* (VF-18, VB-18 and VT-18). Cdr William Ellis, the CO of *Intrepid*'s Carrier Air Group 18, led the combined strike. Most of the naval aviators involved in this mission had never attacked a Japanese warship before, and now they were headed for the largest single surface formation that the IJN had yet employed during the war. The strike took off at 0910hrs and headed west to attack the First Diversion Attack Force some 250 nautical miles away.

As Ellis approached the Japanese force, the size of *Yamato* and *Musashi* stood out – it was not surprising that these ships became the primary focus of his attack. With no IJN aircraft present, the 21 fighters were ordered to strafe the Japanese ships to protect the torpedo-bombers. The 12 Helldivers were ordered to attack *Yamato* and *Musashi* with their 1,000lb bombs, six dive-bombers being dedicated to each ship. The eight *Intrepid* Avengers were allocated the eastern side of Kurita's formation. Two were

Yamato in formation at the beginning of the attack as pictured from an *Intrepid* aircraft. Beginning with the first wave, most naval aviators selected *Musashi* for attack, instead of the equally large *Yamato*. (Naval History and Heritage Command, Photo Archives, Naval Subject Collection)

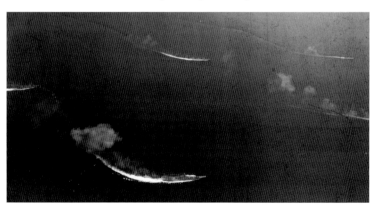

ordered to take on the heavy cruiser *Myoko* that was screening the easternmost Yamato-class battleship. The six remaining torpedo-bombers were sent after the huge battleship, dividing into two three-aircraft sections and approaching the target from its port and starboard bows in a classic anvil attack. The last four Avengers from *Cabot* were assigned to take on the farthest Yamato-class ship.

At about 1000hrs, *Musashi*'s radar picked up the approaching US Navy aircraft. On a clear day, framed between the lush tropical vegetation of Mindoro and Tablas Island, the first ever confrontation between American carrier aircraft and the world's largest battleships was played out. According to Ellis, the engagement commenced as follows:

> The Japs opened up on our formation at very long range, using everything they had, including turret guns, and the cumulative effect was terrific. Pilots [described] some of the AA bursts as pink with streamers, others, purple with white tracer, and an abundance of white phosphorus. One shell that burst ejected silvery pellets.

As the Americans pressed home their attack, *Musashi*'s antiaircraft batteries opened up with what looked to be an impenetrable barrage of fire. The naval aviators continued through the barrage of multicolored 5in. bursts. Closer in, the Helldivers and Avengers came within range of the 25mm guns, which opened up in what appeared to be a stream of light created by the tracers that made up every fourth or fifth round fired.

The Helldivers came in first. Two near misses were scored forward, but these had little effect on the ship. Two more near misses were recorded amidships. Next came the Hellcats, strafing the battleship along its length. The six Avengers delivered the first important blow of the battle by scoring one torpedo hit amidships slightly abaft the bridge on the starboard side. *Musashi*'s air-filled void was unable to deal with the force of the blast, the critical joint failing between the main belt and the lower belt below it. This caused the two belts to shear inward, which led to slow flooding into the adjacent boiler room. The result was a 5.5-degree list, which was reduced to a single degree by pumps in the affected boiler room and counter-flooding on the port side.

During this attack, *Musashi* reported to have fired 48 6.1in. and 60 5in. rounds – a shockingly low amount in the face of a major attack. One Avenger was shot down before it could drop its weapon and a second went down after launching its torpedo. The two Avengers that attacked *Myoko* were even more successful. One torpedo hit the heavy cruiser, forcing it out of the battle and the war. The primary target of the first attack was *Musashi*, however, and its ordeal was just beginning.

The second strike (also from TG 38.2) was launched at 1045hrs, with its attack commencing just after 1200hrs. Some 42 aircraft were involved – 19 Hellcats, 12 Helldivers and 11 Avengers. The attack was well coordinated and was over in only a few minutes. This time, based on advice from Cdr Ellis to the new strike leader, the attack focused solely on *Musashi*. The IJN detected the raid on radar some 50 miles out and prepared for another onslaught.

As usual, the Helldivers came in first. At least two bomb hits were confirmed, along with five near misses. One bomb hit forward and passed through *Musashi*'s bow flare without exploding. The second 1,000lb hit was much more destructive. Striking the ship just to the port side of the stack,

Even though the carrier aircraft focused on *Musashi*, *Yamato* also came under attack and suffered light damage. Here, one of the two 1,000lb bombs that struck the ship explodes forward of Turret No. 1. Note the smoke from the 25mm guns and the wooden deck planking that had been blackened in anticipation of the crew having to fight a night battle while breaking through the San Bernardino Strait. (Naval History and Heritage Command, Photo Archives, Naval Subject Collection)

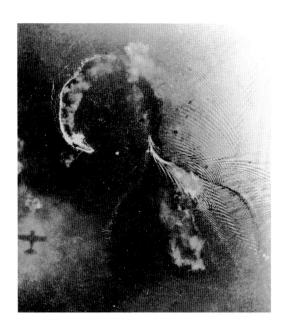

Musashi and an escorting destroyer maneuver to avoid bombs being dropped by aircraft from TG 38.2 during the early stages of the engagement with the First Diversion Attack Force. Note the distinctive Avenger silhouette on a cloud to the left of the photograph. (Barrett Tillman)

it penetrated two decks before probably hitting the main armored deck and exploding. The port side inboard engine room had to be abandoned because of superheated steam entering the space, thus reducing the ship to only three shafts. A fire also broke out near one of the boiler rooms, but this was quickly extinguished. Adding to the confusion and noise, the ship's steam siren was damaged, and it continued to sound off and on for the remainder of the action.

The nine Avengers from *Intrepid* conducted another anvil attack. Of these, eight dropped their weapons. Although accounts vary on the location, it seems three hits were scored on the port side. One torpedo struck the port side near the stack on the junction of the outboard port engine room and the port hydraulic machinery space. This caused slow flooding, but was containable. Another confirmed hit was recorded on the port side just forward of the armored citadel. As was typical on Yamato-class ships, a torpedo hit in this unarmored area flooded several large storerooms. The third hit abaft Turret No. 2, also on the port side. The ship remained on an even keel, but the flooding forward brought the trim down by 6.5ft.

In this attack, *Musashi* reportedly fired 54 Type 3, 17 6.1in. and 200 5in. shells. The ship's impressive volume of fire forced one Avenger to ditch due to damage some 15 miles away and downed two Helldivers. American pilots were impressed that they were engaged with main-battery shells at 25,000–30,000 yards, but no aircraft were damaged.

After two attacks *Musashi* was not in any danger of sinking, and it retained significant combat capabilities. The counter-flooding had reduced its buoyancy reserves, but the ship had only a small list to port. The biggest problem was the reduced speed of 22 knots from only three shafts. In order not to leave *Musashi* behind, Kurita ordered his force to cut its speed to 20 knots, which allowed the ship to regain its place in the formation.

The third raid directed at the First Diversion Attack Force was launched from TG 38.3 at 1250hrs. From USS *Essex* (CV-9) and USS *Lexington* (CV-16) a total of 16 Hellcats (VF-15 from CV-9 and VF-19 from CV-16), 20 Helldivers (VB-15 from CV-9 and VB-19 from CV-16) and 32 Avengers (VT-15 from CV-9 and VT-19 from CV-16) were sent aloft. This attack began at 1330hrs, the aircraft targeting both *Yamato* and *Musashi*. In this round, at least four bombs hit *Musashi*. Three were clustered around the forward 18.1in. turret and penetrated the top deck to explode in the unoccupied crew accommodation spaces below. Damage was not severe and no fires took hold. The last bomb struck the starboard side of the stack and exploded on impact. It devastated nearby 25mm mounts and caused heavy casualties, but did no serious damage.

Much more seriously, a further three torpedo hits were recorded. Two struck on either side of the bow forward of the armored citadel, causing extensive flooding that spread across the entire ship on the middle deck. The hull plating was forced outward by the explosion, leaving the hull looking like a huge plow throwing water up as the ship moved forward. Another hit on the starboard side close to the previous starboard hit increased the flooding and forced the starboard hydraulic machinery room to be abandoned. There was possibly a third hit in the area of the forward 6.1in. triple turret on the starboard side, but this cannot be confirmed.

Yet despite this pounding, the list was only increased to two degrees to starboard. Additional counter-flooding reduced this. However, the ship's speed now dropped to 16 knots, which meant that *Musashi* slowly fell behind Kurita's formation. This was further reduced by Inoguchi to 12 knots, as he feared that the ship could be plunged beneath the surface of the water by the bow. The freeboard of 32.8ft on the bow was now down to 19.6ft, and the ship was drawing 50ft.

Damage from seven torpedo and six bomb hits would likely have sunk any other battleship, and even *Musashi* could not take this kind of pounding and stay in action. Kurita ordered the ship to proceed to the west with two destroyers. Even with all this damage, the battleship was in no immediate danger of sinking, since there was no progressive flooding.

Musashi maneuvers under attack from *Intrepid* aircraft during the second strike from the carrier. The lack of escorts is noteworthy, reflecting IJN doctrine that ships were expected to maneuver independently when under air attack. Also noteworthy is the virtual lack of shell bursts from 5in. fire. (Naval History and Heritage Command, Photo Archives, Naval Subject Collection)

The next raid was the biggest of the day – 65 aircraft launched from USS *Enterprise* (CV-6) and USS *Franklin* (CV-13) of TG 38.4 at about 1315hrs. This force consisted of 26 Hellcats (14 from VF-13 on board CV-13 and 12 from VF-20 embarked in CV-6), 21 Helldivers (12 from VB-13 on board CV-13 and nine from VB-20 embarked in CV-6) and 18 Avengers (ten from VT-13 on board CV-13 and eight from VT-20 embarked in CV-6).

By the time the American aircraft resumed their attack, Kurita had temporarily turned to the west and *Musashi* was on its own. More than half of the strike force went after the crippled battleship, with the remaining aircraft targeting Kurita's main body. *Musashi* was now unable to defend itself, with its speed reduced to 12 knots and only about a quarter of its antiaircraft guns remaining in action. The ship was also unable to maneuver, which made it an easy target.

As previously noted, aircraft from CV-6's Carrier Air Group 20 made up the bulk of the attacking force, which went after *Musashi*. While the fighters were assigned to suppress the escorting destroyers, the Helldiver and Avenger pilots pressed their attacks in as far as possible in order to guarantee hits. The results on the near-defenseless battleship were devastating. The naval aviators claimed that 11 of the 18 Helldivers that dove on *Musashi* scored a hit. For once, these claims were accurate. Within minutes, *Musashi* received ten hits from 1,000lb bombs. The SB2Cs came in over the bow and seemed to be concentrating on the forward superstructure. It must be pointed out that none of the bombs penetrated to vital parts of the ship, which meant that its propulsion and buoyancy remained unaffected.

Going from bow to stern, it is possible to recount the carnage with some degree of certainty. One bomb hit in front of the forward 18.1in. turret and added to the damage caused in earlier attacks. Another bomb hit the roof of the forward turret, although this only created a small depression against the 10.6in. armor. Another hit the starboard side of the forward turret and penetrated two decks before exploding against the 9in. armor in this area. Two bombs hit in the same place slightly to starboard between the forward

OVERLEAF *Musashi* comes under attack from an SB2C-3 Helldiver from VB-18 on October 24, 1944. In order to deliver his weapon accurately, a dive-bomber pilot would hold his release until the aircraft was 1,500–2,000ft above the target. The 1,000lb bomb being dropped could not cripple a heavily-armored battleship, especially one as well protected as *Musashi*, but it could devastate antiaircraft guns and their crews located on the weather decks, which would make the coordinated attacks by Avenger torpedo-bombers more effective. This is exactly what happened to *Musashi*. As many as 16 bomb hits reduced the ship's antiaircraft capabilities to such an extent that Avengers in the last two attacks went in virtually unopposed.

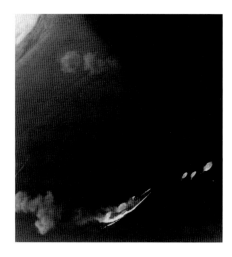

Musashi is targeted by Helldivers from TG 38.3 – this was the third raid generated against the super battleship. A fire started by an earlier dive-bombing attack is clearly burning aft, generating significant amounts of smoke. (Naval History and Heritage Command, Photo Archives, Naval Subject Collection)

Photographed following the Yap Island strike on November 24, 1944, this veteran SB2C-3 of VB-20 had participated in the strikes on *Musashi* the previous month. Indeed, aircraft from *Enterprise*'s Carrier Air Group 20 made up the bulk of the attacking force. (Tailhook)

6.1in. turret and the superstructure, exploding on contact. Another two hit to port in the same general area, but these penetrated two decks until exploding when they struck the 7.9in.-thick armored deck. The eighth bomb hit the port side of the superstructure and exploded on contact. This inflicted great carnage on the nearby 25mm mounts and their crews.

The superstructure also came in for more damage when a bomb hit the top of the tower. This destroyed the main battery fire control director and its rangefinder. The explosion also caused significant casualties on the bridge and in the operations room, with 78 sailors being killed or wounded. Among the latter was Inoguchi, who was hit in his shoulder by shrapnel. He was led to his at-sea cabin and the Executive Officer, Capt Kenkichi Kato, took over. The last hit landed on the centerline abaft the superstructure but caused only minor damage. In addition, there were six near misses that further reduced underwater integrity.

Much more devastating than the barrage of 1,000lb bombs was the continued assault on *Musashi*'s underwater defenses. The US Navy claimed that of the eight *Enterprise* Avengers that attacked – four on each bow – all eight scored hits. It is impossible to state with certainty how many torpedoes struck the battleship, but the total starts with four confirmed hits. Some Japanese sources stated as many as ten found their target. From this point in the action, the accounts given by *Musashi*'s survivors become unreliable, and some of the hits may actually have come during the last attack of the day by *Intrepid* aircraft.

Again, from bow to stern, the first hit was on the port side in the area of the magazine for Turret No. 1. Flooding was soon reported on the two lowest levels of the magazine. Another hit to port was confirmed abeam the superstructure, which caused one boiler room to flood. A second hit to port was recorded just aft of the stack. This was in the immediate area of an earlier torpedo strike, and it caused the port outboard engine room to flood immediately. The effect of these three hits on the port side of the ship was partially alleviated by a confirmed hit on the starboard side in the area of Turret No. 2.

Both Kato and the Chief Engineer, Captain Nakanmura, survived the attack, but their accounts are spotty in parts, clearly erroneous in others, and contradictory. They do not even match up with the times of the attacks as reported by US Navy records. In addition to the four confirmed torpedo hits, there could have been six more possible strikes, for Kato stated three more occurred forward, two to port and one to starboard. Another probable hit was reported to port in the area just forward of Turret No. 3. Two more were said to have struck on the port side amidships, but did not explode. An indication of the ineffectiveness of *Musashi*'s defenses at this point was the fact that all of

This poor-quality but dramatic shot of *Musashi* shows it markedly down by the bow. The ship remains on an even keel, but will soon sink due to progressive flooding. (Naval History and Heritage Command, Photo Archives, Naval Subject Collection)

Enterprise's aircraft returned safely.

The final attack of the day was the third strike from *Intrepid* and *Cabot*. This attack group included 16 Hellcats, 12 Helldivers and three Avengers. By then VT-18 had only four Avengers still operable, and one of these was forced to abort shortly after taking off. This was testimony to the dense Japanese antiaircraft fire throughout the day. The group was launched at 1350hrs and attacked at 1550hrs on the heels of TG 38.4's strike. Cdr Ellis again led the mission, which caused little if any additional damage to *Musashi*.

The attack by *Enterprise's* aircraft left no doubt that the super battleship would sink. Damage now totaled a minimum of 16 bomb and probably 15 torpedo hits. The list increased to 10–12 degrees and the bow was down by another 6.5 feet. Only the starboard shaft was still operational, and top speed had been reduced to 6 knots. Nakanmura ordered the outer three starboard boiler rooms flooded, and this drastic measure stopped the list at 12 degrees. In this condition, at 1715hrs, Kurita ordered *Musashi* to beach itself on nearby Sibuyan Island. This was clearly impossible since *Musashi* could barely move on its remaining single shaft and the flooding could not be stopped. Down by the bow, the ship would not answer to its helm, so it circled slowly. By 1800hrs flooding had forced the last boiler room to be abandoned, which left the ship without power.

At 1900hrs the final phase began. The list increased and reached 15 degrees. Down by the bow, the sea reached the port side of Turret No. 1. By 1920hrs the list had reached 30 degrees. This prompted Kato to give the order to abandon ship. *Musashi's* massive stern rose as the bow sank deeper, and then it began a slow roll to port. Finally, the ship turned bottom up and then slid under, bow first. By 1936hrs, it was gone. Three destroyers plucked 1,376 survivors from the water, but 1,023 sailors were lost, including Inoguchi, who elected to go down with his ship.

Yamato and the remaining units of the First Diversion Attack Force came under attack on October 26 while retreating through the Sibuyan Sea. This is a fine overhead shot of *Yamato* taken at 1115hrs from 10,000ft by a B-24 Liberator from the 424th BS/307th BG. (Naval History and Heritage Command, Photo Archives, Naval Subject Collection)

YAMATO'S FINAL SORTIE

Following the battle of Leyte Gulf, *Yamato* returned to Japan in the first week of December. The ship had taken two bomb hits forward from SB2C-3s of VB-15 (embarked in *Essex*) on October 24. A third bomb had also struck forward of Turret No. 1 two days later – this was dropped by a Helldiver from VB-11, embarked in USS *Hornet* (CV-12). The damage inflicted on the

Operation *Ten-Go* was a senseless venture with little hope of success. With a small task force of one light cruiser and eight destroyers, *Yamato* was ordered to leave the Inland Sea and head to Okinawa to attack the US Navy's invasion force more than 500 nautical miles distant. Since no air cover was provided, *Yamato*'s only hope of achieving this dubious mission was gaining the element of surprise. This was unlikely given US air superiority. As soon as the *Yamato* force put to sea it was spotted by American aircraft and then again by American submarines as it departed the Inland Sea. On the morning of April 7, 1945, the IJN ships were tracked by Mariner flying boats and Hellcat fighters, which guided in three waves of attacking aircraft from the US Navy carrier force operating east of Okinawa. Less then two hours after the start of the attack *Yamato* blew up, still some 200 miles short of its objective.

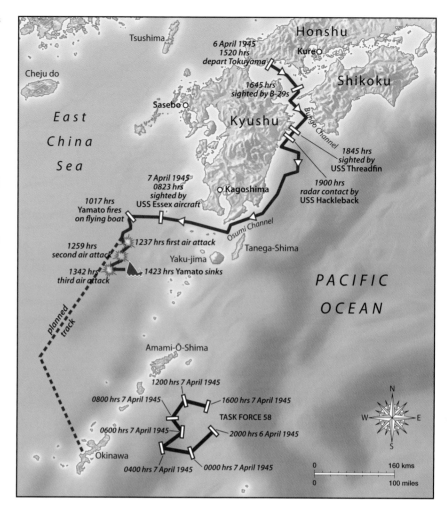

24th caused 3,000 tons of water to enter the ship, while the bomb two days later heavily damaged the forward armored bulkhead.

After repairs had been carried out, the ship was attacked in the Inland Sea by US Navy carrier aircraft on March 19, 1945. Although the *Yamato* was undamaged, clearly the IJN could no longer hide its sole remaining super battleship from marauding American carrier aircraft.

The April 1 American landing on Okinawa demanded a strong Japanese response. A massive air assault had been pre-planned for such an eventuality, and this was scheduled for April 6. Originally, there was no surface ship component to the operation, which had been designated *Ten-Go* (Heaven Operation). By April 4, however, the commander of the Combined Fleet was convinced that *Yamato* should be added to *Ten-Go*. It takes a certain insight into the Japanese mindset, particularly that prevailing within the staff of the Combined Fleet, to understand why such an operation was even considered. With *Yamato* already vulnerable to air attack, and American forces on Japan's doorstep, it was unthinkable that the symbol of the IJN would not seek action while the nation struggled for survival.

Using *Yamato* as a spectacular kamikaze would protect the honor of the IJN, shelter it from charges of cowardice from the Imperial Army and answer the Emperor's query on

March 29 as to why no surface ships had been included in *Ten-Go*. Once decided, *Yamato*'s sortie to support the defenders of Okinawa was quickly planned and ordered on April 5. A lack of fuel meant that only a few ships could be allocated to the mission. For *Ten-Go*, the Second Fleet could muster a total of ten warships. The heart of the force was *Yamato*, and it was escorted by the light cruiser *Yahagi* and the destroyers *Asashimo*, *Fuyutsuki*, *Hamakaze*, *Hatsushimo*, *Isokaze*, *Kasumi*, *Suzutsuki* and *Yukikaze*. The force was commanded by Vice Admiral Seiichi Ito, with Capt Kosaku Aruga as the commanding officer of *Yamato*.

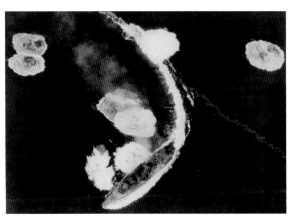

Yamato maneuvers whilst coming under heavy attack from US Navy carrier aircraft in the Inland Sea on March 19, 1945. Near misses such as those seen here could cause considerable damage if loosened plates resulted in flooding, although on this occasion the ship was not damaged. This photograph was taken by Helldivers from VB-17, embarked in *Hornet*. (Naval History and Heritage Command, Photo Archives, Naval Subject Collection)

The plan was an exercise in fantasy. *Yamato* was to reach the area of the invasion and then destroy the enemy fleet there. If necessary, the super battleship was to be run aground and its guns used to support the Japanese garrison. *Yamato* was not allocated any air cover for the relatively short trip to Okinawa. Unless surprise could be achieved, which was unlikely given the number of American aircraft available, the prospects of *Yamato* reaching Okinawa were remote. Although not formally framed as a suicide mission, it was acknowledged that it was unlikely *Yamato* would return. The entire undertaking was simply a ceremonial vehicle for the destruction of the IJN's last remaining symbol, rather than a serious plan with a hope of making a contribution toward victory. It was yet another display of the bankrupt strategic planning then so prevalent within the IJN.

On April 6, *Yamato* fueled at the Tokuyama naval oil depot. Despite the prevailing myth that the ship and its escorts had only enough fuel for a one-way trip, the authorities at Tokuyama issued 4,000 tons of fuel to *Yamato*, which was enough for a round trip. It departed Tokuyama Bay at 1518hrs and headed for the Bungo Strait. One-third of the crew was at battle stations, with the remainder sleeping near their stations because of the threat of submarine or air attack.

Before dark, the force was sighted by two American bombers. The next challenge was getting through the Bungo Strait, where US Navy submarines were known to patrol. The transit was uneventful, even though at 2240hrs one of the escorting destroyers reported the presence of a submarine. In fact, the force had been detected by two submarines, USS *Threadfin* (SS-410) and USS *Hackleback* (SS-295). The Japanese intercepted the submarines' sighting report, so there was no doubt that the Americans were aware of the operation. Prudence would have demanded that the loss of surprise cancel the operation, but the IJN was not of that mind. With no air cover planned for the next day, the fate of *Yamato* was certain.

At 0700hrs on April 7 the crew was given a ceremonial breakfast and then ordered to prepare for battle. They did not have long to wait before engaging the enemy. At 1000hrs two Martin PBM Mariner flying boats appeared over the fleet and began to shadow it. These were soon joined by Hellcats, which were part of a group of 40 fighters launched from TF 58 in groups of four to search out to 325 nautical miles. As the crew went to battle stations, all doors and hatches were closed and the ventilation system secured. *Yamato* unsuccessfully engaged the shadowing American aircraft with three salvos of *San-Shiki* shells from its 18.1in. guns.

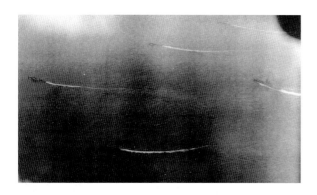

Even before *Yamato* had been firmly located, TF 58 began to launch a massive strike. A total of 386 aircraft were sent aloft from 15 carriers. Aircraft from five of the carriers failed to find the target in the bad weather, or arrived too late to take part in the attack. The actual number of attacking aircraft was 227. TG 58.1 was first to launch at 1000hrs with 113 aircraft – 52 fighters, 21 dive-bombers and 40 torpedo-bombers. It was followed by TG 58.3 with 167 aircraft – 80 fighters, 29 dive-bombers and 58 torpedo-bombers. The last to launch was TG 58.4 at about 1045hrs with 106 aircraft – 48 fighters, 25 dive-bombers and 33 torpedo-bombers – many of which were late reaching the target. The weather made locating the Japanese force difficult, but most of the attackers were guided to the ships by the shadowing aircraft. Helldiver and Avenger crews were aided in final homing by the radar equipment fitted to their aircraft.

Yamato in formation with four destroyers, photographed by an aircraft launched from *Bennington*. This shot was taken just prior to the first attack at about 1230hrs. (Naval History and Heritage Command, Photo Archives, Naval Subject Collection)

The 15 SB2C-4Es assigned to VB-82 on board *Bennington* saw plenty of action from late January through to June 1945. Four Helldivers from the unit were the first to attack *Yamato* on April 7, these aircraft placing two bombs around the mainmast on the starboard side and destroying a 5in. gun mount. The bombs blew a large hole in the weather deck. One Helldiver was downed by flak in return. (US Navy)

With American aircraft detected in the area, *Yamato* went to 24 knots. The poor weather, with a cloud base as low as 3,000ft, and the large size of the strike made coordination difficult. On a more positive note for the naval aviators, the low cloud cover meant that *Yamato* struggled to effectively employ its antiaircraft defenses. This was primarily because the fire control directors lacked the time to obtain a fire solution on American aircraft diving out of the clouds. The desired barrage was never achieved and central control of the antiaircraft battery was abandoned in favor of local control.

What ensued for the next, almost two hours will never be fully reconstructed. The relevant Japanese records did not survive the war and only a handful of credible accounts have emerged. The best of these come from a handful of survivors interrogated by the US Navy after the war.

The attack proceeded in sequence, with aircraft from TG 58.1 coming in first. The initial wave was detected by *Yamato*'s radar at 1220hrs to the southeast, and some 12 minutes later the first American aircraft were spotted eight miles away. The first group to attack, at 1237hrs, came from USS *Bennington* (CV-20) when four Helldivers (from VB-82) approached from astern, where the antiaircraft protection was the weakest. These aircraft placed two bombs around the mainmast on the starboard side and destroyed a 5in. gun mount. The bombs exploded on contact and blew a large hole in the weather deck. In addition, several 25mm mounts in the area were also destroyed. One of the attacking aircraft was shot down.

Fourteen Helldivers from VB-17, embarked in *Hornet*, were next in. Within minutes,

another two bombs hit slightly to port just forward of the aft 6.1in. triple turret. Both of the bombs penetrated to the main armored deck, where they exploded. The fires spread to the shell handling areas below the 6.1in. turret and ignited the ready-use powder, killing all but a single member of the gun crew. The flash doors to the magazine stopped the fire from getting any further, however. The explosion and fire also killed the damage control party responsible for the area, and the blaze continued to burn throughout the battle. Additionally, the aft radar control room and a number of 25mm mounts were destroyed.

Yamato under attack by *Hornet* aircraft during the first strike. Only three destroyers are left to protect the super battleship and the relative paucity of bursts from Japanese 5in. guns is evident. A torpedo or bomb has just exploded forward on the starboard side. (Naval History and Heritage Command, Photo Archives, Naval Subject Collection)

More devastating than the destruction wrought by the bombs were the first torpedo hits. One of the Avenger pilots from VT-17, also embarked in *Hornet*, described the attack:

> One aircraft radioed that he had seen a blip [on his radar screen] off to starboard about 50 miles out, so we turned right. Then we saw them. Holy mackerel! *Yamato* looked like the Empire State Building plowing through the water.
>
> We didn't have too much ceiling. I was at 12,000ft at most, and usually liked to start at 18,000ft for a torpedo run – a steep approach, then tight over the water to drop the torpedo, before getting the hell out of there. Meanwhile, the bombers were supposed to be going down, so we all hit the ship simultaneously.
>
> We spread out, and I kept diving toward different puffs of smoke where shells had already exploded – there shouldn't have been any damage there. I went down, dropped my torpedo and went right across the bow of *Yamato*. The ship was turning, but in our attack we always dropped in a fan shape, so no matter which way a ship was turning, it was going to get hit.

The group of eight Avengers from *Hornet* approached from *Yamato*'s port side. One lesson learned from the *Musashi* episode was to concentrate all torpedo hits on a single side to hasten the ship's demise. Of the eight aircraft, six were hit on their attack runs and one crashed into the water without dropping its weapon. The other seven launched a spread against *Yamato*, and four ran straight and true – the Americans claimed all four hit. One struck just abaft the bridge and another just abaft the mainmast. Another probable torpedo hit abaft Turret No. 3. Some survivors stated that a fourth torpedo hit during this attack, but this cannot be confirmed. These strikes flooded the outboard voids and caused a port list of 5–6 degrees, but this was corrected to only one degree by counter-flooding. *Yamato* remained in fighting shape, with its speed unimpaired.

While *Yamato* was getting hammered, *Hamakaze* was hit by a torpedo from a *Bennington*-based Avenger from VT-82 and quickly sank. TBM-1C/3s from VT-45, embarked in the light carrier USS *San Jacinto* (CVL-30), finished off *Asashimo* in minutes with a combined bomb and torpedo attack. *Yahagi* was also hit amidships by a single torpedo and crippled.

At 1259hrs the second wave from TG 58.3 arrived, consisting of aircraft from *Essex*, USS *Bunker Hill* (CV-17), and light carriers USS *Bataan* (CVL-29) and *Cabot*. The strike group (VB-6 and VT-6) from USS *Hancock* (CV-19) launched late and then got lost, so it never made an attack. VB-83's Helldivers from *Essex* went in first, diving from 6,200ft. Despite American claims to the contrary, apparently no direct bomb hits were made, but the Avengers continued their torpedo assault on *Yamato*'s port side. The attack by 15 TBM-3/3Es from *Essex* was

Avengers from VT-82 sank the destroyer *Hamakaze* during the action that also saw the end of *Yamato*. Note the strike camera fixed to the fuselage in front of the cockpit on the TBM in the foreground. These aircraft were photographed on a patrol from *Bennington* shortly after April 7, 1945. (Pete Clayton)

particularly effective, the last nine closing in on their target in "a perfect setup for the shot" as *Yamato* made a slow turn. Nine hits were claimed. VT-84 from *Bunker Hill* also claimed nine hits from 13 torpedoes dropped, while *Cabot*'s Avenger crews (from VT-29) claimed four more. In total, TG 58.3 torpedo pilots claimed 29 hits.

In fact, only three were confirmed – one abeam the stack, the next abeam the bridge and another forward of the stack. Another probable hit occurred on the port side in the area of the mainmast. There was also a confirmed hit on the starboard side in the area of the bridge at 1309hrs. This was the work of VT-47's nine Avengers from *Bataan*. This torpedo barrage created a list to port of 15–16 degrees, although this was reduced to 5 degrees by counter-flooding and the effect of the starboard side torpedo hit. To accomplish this, however, all starboard side voids were used. Speed was reduced to 18 knots because of the inrush of water and the loss of one propeller shaft. At this point *Yamato*'s damage was massive, but not mortal.

On board the super battleship, the crew fought furiously against the relentless air attacks. As previously noted, the same low overcast cloud that prevented the Americans from conducting full dives also prevented the fire control equipment from gaining a fire control solution. The gun mounts fought in local control against whatever targets

Yamato maneuvers frantically under attack as a bomb explodes off its port side. The fire in the area of the aft 6.1in. turret can be clearly seen. Note the smoke from the 25mm triple mounts. (Naval History and Heritage Command, Photo Archives, Naval Subject Collection)

presented themselves. By the second attack only half of the gun crews remained active, the strafing of the Hellcats and the bombs from the Helldivers proving to be brutally effective as they created carnage above decks. The gun crews were unprotected and thus suffered terrible casualties. As the engagement raged above them, the damage control crews fought a losing battle to keep the ship on an even keel.

At 1342hrs the final attack began, this time from TG 58.4 featuring aircraft from *Intrepid*, USS *Yorktown* (CV-10) and the light carrier USS *Langley* (CVL-27). Fourteen Helldivers from VB-10, embarked in *Intrepid*, led off, but again bomb damage seems to have been fairly minor. Possibly three bombs hit the port side amidships, but these exploded on contact and did no serious damage.

Much more serious was the continued torpedo assault. Two torpedo hits (claimed by Lt Cdr Herbert Houck's VT-9, which had sortied from *Yorktown*) were confirmed on the port side, one near the stack and another near the mainmast. These resulted in the flooding of the inboard engine room and port side boiler room and the loss of another propeller shaft. A witness account of a torpedo hitting the port side just forward of Turret No. 3 cannot be confirmed. Another hit was confirmed on the starboard side in the area of the mainmast. With no reserve capacity to conduct counter-flooding, the crew was helpless to prevent the list increasing to 16–18 degrees. Nevertheless, the two remaining outer starboard side boiler rooms and the hydraulic machinery room on the starboard side were flooded to compensate. This had the temporary effect of stopping the list from increasing further.

The progressive flooding could not be checked, however. The second starboard side torpedo hit caused flooding in the outboard starboard engine room, which was soon abandoned and then flooded. Progressive flooding was also reported in the inboard port engine room. At this point the list to port increased to 22–23 degrees and speed was reduced to 8 knots on a single shaft. The ship could now only steam in a large circle.

Shortly after 1400hrs all power was lost. The end was now only a matter of time, as *Yamato* lay dead in the water with its port side awash. The list could no longer be contained, and was increasing, so Capt Aruga ordered the crew to abandon ship. It was too late. Soon after the order was given the ship began to capsize – by 1420hrs, *Yamato* was on its beam ends. When the roll reached 120 degrees, a huge explosion in the area of the aft magazine tore the ship to pieces. At 1423hrs the world's most famous battleship sank below the waves. Only 276 men were saved from topside battle stations, some 3,055 having perished. Their watery grave was marked by a column of smoke that reached a height of almost 20,000 ft, allowing it to be seen in Japan some 120 miles away.

The source of the explosion remains unclear. The ship's Executive Officer, Capt Jiro Nomura, blamed it on the detonation of the 18.1in. shells when the ship rolled over and their fuses hit the deck. Postwar tests indicated that this could not have been the reason, however. The fire aft seems a more likely cause. When the ship turned over, the hoists from the magazine could have been opened by the weight of the 18.1in. projectiles, and fire entered the magazine in that manner. Surveys of *Yamato*'s wreck conducted in 1985 and shortly thereafter confirm that the forward part is fairly intact back to the area of the forward 6.1in. turret, but that the middle of the ship back to its intact stern section was shattered.

Joining *Yamato* on the bottom of the East China Sea was *Yahagi* and four of the eight destroyers. Casualties were particularly heavy on the light cruiser, which was literally blown apart. A total of 1,187 men died on the escort ships.

Yamato blows up at about 1423hrs on April 7, 1945, after being subjected to intense air attack by American carrier aircraft. The immense pillar of smoke marked the end of the battleship era and the IJN. (Naval History and Heritage Command)

STATISTICS AND ANALYSIS

The destruction of the battleship *Hiei* on November 14, 1942 gave the US Navy a taste of how difficult it was to sink heavily armored warships with aircraft. Although modernized, *Hiei* was a design dating from before World War I. It was also less than half the displacement of *Yamato* and *Musashi*. Nevertheless, in the two encounters between carrier aircraft and the world's biggest battleships, the clear winner was naval air power.

It took massive attacks by multiple carrier air groups to sink the IJN's largest ships. Both were eventually dispatched with torpedoes. Bombs did not contribute significantly to the sinking of the battleships, but they did reduce the effectiveness of their antiaircraft defenses and thus contributed to the effectiveness of the torpedo-bomber attacks.

The strikes on the First Diversion Attack Force in October 1944 represented the largest air–sea battle in history up to that point. The 29 ships of Kurita's force were subjected to a series of attacks by 259 carrier aircraft. For the loss of 18 aircraft, the US Navy sank *Musashi*, torpedoed the heavy cruiser *Myoko* and forced it back to base, and inflicted minor bomb damage on three other battleships. Clearly this was an American victory, but several issues deserve to be examined more closely.

The most obvious conclusion was that *Musashi* showed itself to be able to absorb amazing punishment in excess of what its designers called for. Even after the first three attacks, *Musashi* could have returned to port. The fourth attack, when it was virtually unprotected and unable to maneuver, was the ship's death knell. No other warship in history had taken as much damage – at least 11 and as many as 15 torpedoes and 16 bomb hits, plus many near misses. No other ship then afloat could have survived this type of punishment.

Secondly, Japanese antiaircraft defenses were ineffective. Only 6.9 percent of the US Navy aircraft attacking the heaviest concentration of IJN antiaircraft batteries of the entire war were lost. The Type 3 antiaircraft shell designed for the 18.1in. gun was totally ineffective. For doctrinal reasons, the Type 89 5in. guns were used on a limited basis only. This left the main defense to the inaccurate and light 25mm weapons.

From another perspective, the 250+ sorties mounted by TF 38 against the First Diversion Attack Force bought the US Navy a relatively poor return. In this respect, *Musashi* performed a valuable service to the Japanese plan, since most of the carrier air group attacks of October 24 were focused on a single target. This was largely because there was not a single coordinator for the American air strikes, which came in by individual carrier air group. Each of these sought a spectacular target, and *Musashi* was clearly one of the two largest available. Once it was damaged and clearly down by the bows or moving slowly by itself away from the main formation, the temptation to finish the ship off was clearly irresistible.

The effect was that *Musashi* absorbed the bulk of the strikes launched by TF 38 that day. While it was getting pounded under the waves, the other primary Japanese ships of the First Diversionary Attack Force suffered little damage. *Yamato* and *Nagato* received two bombs each and the battleship *Haruna* easily withstood five near misses, and all three were able to remain in formation.

The naval aviators involved saw it differently, however. They reported that *both* Yamato-class battleships had been crippled, with one probably sunk, *Nagato* had also been hit and badly damaged, and a Kongo-class battleship crippled. In addition, as many as four heavy cruisers, two light cruisers and six destroyers were reported sunk or damaged. Such losses could only mean that Kurita's force had been crippled. When the last US Navy strike left the area, the Japanese force was milling around and apparently getting ready to retire. This total misreading of the situation by naval aviators led to the most dramatic phases of the battle of Leyte Gulf. Based on these reports, Halsey chased after the Japanese carrier force the next day, which allowed Kurita to transit through the San Bernardino Strait and head south to Leyte. None of this would have happened as it did without *Musashi*'s capability to absorb unparalleled punishment and the American decision to focus primarily on a single tempting target.

By the time of the *Yamato* sortie, the US Navy had learned some important lessons. Each of its carrier air groups launched to strike *Yamato* had a coordinator. This solved the problem of over-concentration on a single target. More importantly, the Avenger squadrons aimed their torpedoes at one side of the massive battleship only. Even so, *Yamato* was able to absorb nine to 12 torpedo and seven bomb hits. By comparison,

Armorers from VB-14 prepare to load a 1,000lb AN-Mk 33 armor-piercing bomb into the bomb-bay of a Helldiver on board USS *Wasp* (CV-18) in 1944. This weapon was distinguished by its cone-shaped nose, the AN-Mk 33 being reserved for attacking heavily armored warships. There were also 500 and 1,000lb semi-armor-piercing bombs and general purpose bombs that contained lighter casings and more explosives – the latter were available in 100, 250, 500, 1,000, and 2,000lb sizes, and they could all be carried by the Helldiver and the Avenger. (Real War Photos)

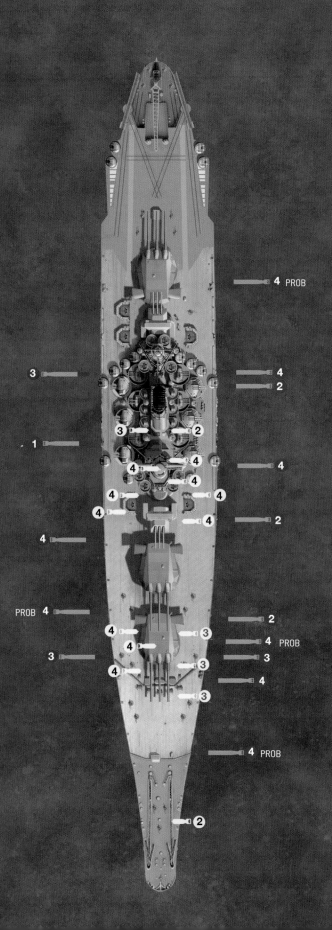

For more than five hours on October 24, 1944, *Musashi* came under intense aerial attack. A definitive accounting of the damage it received during this period is not possible, but the totals given in this diagram take into account US Navy reports and Japanese survivor accounts. It is clear that between 11 and 15 torpedoes were needed to sink the ship. The large number was due to *Musashi*'s sheer size and heavy armor, the crew's excellent damage control work and the fact that the torpedo hits were distributed on both sides of the ship, which helped control the port list where the majority of the damage occurred. The large number of bomb hits did not threaten *Musashi*'s watertight integrity, but they did degrade the ship's antiaircraft battery, making it easier for the torpedo-bombers to do their work.

Diagram of battle damage to battleship *Musashi*
24 October 1945

First attack
1 torpedo

Second attack
3 torpedoes, 2 bombs

Third attack
3 torpedoes, 4 bombs

Fourth attack
8 torpedoes (4 confirmed, 4 probable)
10 bombs

Total
16 bombs
15 torpedoes

Compared to their attack on *Musashi* the previous October, naval aviators were more efficient in their assault on *Yamato* in April 1945. As seen in this damage diagram, the three attacks focused on the battleship's port side, which quickly created a list and eventually caused the ship to capsize. Most of the torpedo damage was concentrated on the same area of the armored citadel that defeated *Yamato*'s anti-torpedo defenses. The second attack was particularly deadly since it accounted for three confirmed and another probable torpedo hit on the port side. As with *Musashi*, the exact number of hits will never be known. Because of the bad weather that affected accurate dive-bombing, *Yamato* only suffered some seven bomb hits.

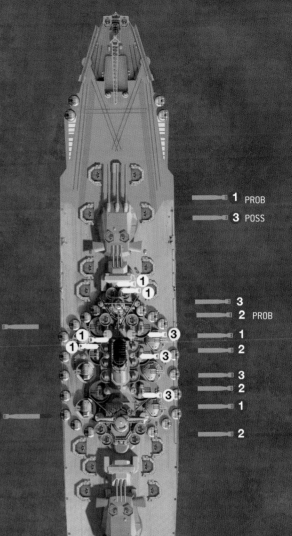

1 PROB
3 POSS

3
2 PROB
1
2
3
2
1
2

Diagram of battle damage to battleship *Yamato*
1 April 1945

First attack
4 bombs, 3 torpedoes (2 confirmed, 1 probable)

Second attack
5 torpedoes (4 confirmed, 1 probable)

Third attack
3 bombs, 4 torpedoes (3 confirmed, 1 possible)

Total
7 bombs
9–12 torpedoes

American losses were a meager ten aircraft (four Helldivers, three Hellcats and three Avengers) and 12 aircrew lost (four pilots and eight crew).

The sacrifice of *Yamato* was pointless. If its mission had been coordinated with kamikaze attacks on TF 58, then the ship's final sortie could have had some value. As it was, only 54 kamikaze aircraft were launched on April 7, and only half of those found a target.

To be fair, no ships of the period could have survived the damage incurred by either *Yamato* or *Musashi*, but there were faults in the designs of these ships that contributed to their loss. The principal weakness was in their anti-torpedo defenses. The problem was two-fold – the defective joint joining the armor of the upper and lower belts and the system of void compartments in the blisters. The IJN knew there was a problem with the side armor joints but elected not to address it because it would have slowed delivery of the ships. The effectiveness of the void system could have been improved if these spaces had been filled with fluid, as was the case in other navies, since this would have increased resistance to underwater explosions. The IJN placed great importance on counter-flooding to reduce the effects of torpedo damage, but here too its design was less then optimal. With a severe list, counter-flooding and the pumping system it relied on could only fill the outboard void of the undamaged side of the ship to 55 percent of capacity.

Finally, the super battleships' unarmored bow area was also a cause for concern. Once damaged, extensive flooding resulted, adversely affecting trim. The problem here was excessively large compartments.

When designing the Yamato-class ships, the IJN failed to reckon on the development of a torpedo armed with 600lb of Torpex (which had more destructive power than TNT). This delivered an explosive force much larger than the battleships' anti-torpedo defenses had been designed to deal with. Even with the enormous weight of *Yamato* and *Musashi*, compromises had to be made. No ship could be armored enough to withstand a relentless pounding like that which the US Navy was capable of dealing out in 1944–45.

This is *Yamato* under attack on October 25, 1944 – the day after the massive attacks in the Sibuyan Sea. Here, an Avenger from VC-20, embarked in the escort carrier USS *Kadashan Bay* (CVE-76), approaches the battleship off Samar at an altitude of 1,500ft. This photograph gives a good feel for the perspective faced by a torpedo-bomber pilot. (Naval History and Heritage Command, Photo Archives, Naval Subject Collection)

AFTERMATH

The sinking of *Yamato* brought a symbolic end to the era of the battleship, its demise, along with the destruction of its sister ship *Musashi*, proving that there was no such thing as an unsinkable capital ship.

Yamato proved to be a disastrous investment, as feared by some in the IJN before it was built. It never fired at a US Navy battleship like it had been designed to do. During the ship's short and unproductive career, *Yamato* only fired its 18.1in. main battery at a single target – an insignificant US Navy escort carrier off Samar on October 25, 1944. There is also some doubt as to whether the super battleship's gunners hit what they were aiming for.

The final battle of *Yamato* was particularly noteworthy for its futility. Unable to defend itself, the ship was sunk by US Navy carrier air power for only trifling American losses. Even the notion that *Yamato* would draw the attention of the Pacific Fleet carriers towards it, and therefore ease the path of Japanese suicide aircraft, proved faulty. With the ship's demise, the IJN became almost totally reliant on suicide attacks against the American invasion force in the planned occupation of Japan.

Musashi gave a good account of itself and demonstrated how tough it was to sink the world's most heavily armored ship. At least its death offered a valuable contribution to the Japanese war effort, since the American attacks on October 24 in the Sibuyan Sea focused primarily on the super battleship. This in turn allowed the rest of the First Diversion Attack Force to transit with minimal losses into the Philippine Sea, providing the Japanese with the illusion of victory the following day. However, as has been made clear, even if the First Diversion Attack Force had broken into Leyte Gulf, it would have accomplished nothing significant. In exchange, it is all but certain that Kurita's entire force would have been trapped and destroyed. The ships and men of the First Diversion Attack Force deserved a plan more worthy of their sacrifice.

This photograph shows the heavy cruiser *Kumano* under attack by Helldivers dropping 1,000lb bombs on October 26, 1944, as the First Diversion Attack Force withdraw through the Sibuyan Sea. The engagement took place in the Tablas Strait near the southern tip of Mindoro Island. Japanese sources indicate that three bombs (500 pounders – if true, then these were from the 12 F6F Hellcats that participated in the strike) hit the ship, causing severe damage. None of the TBM-1C torpedo-bombers that attacked scored a torpedo hit. The cruiser was able to reach port and make repairs, providing another example of the difficulty in sinking heavy ships with bombs alone. (Real War Photos)

For the Americans, the carrier came out of the war as the centerpiece of the US Navy. This status of the carrier remained unchanged through the Cold War and even up to the present time. The demise of the battleship also meant the end of the torpedo-bomber. The postwar careers of the Avenger and Helldiver were relatively short, with fighter-bombers such as the F4U Corsair taking center stage due to their versatility. New strike aircraft like the AD Skyraider, designed without the restrictions that bedeviled the Helldiver, proved to be far more capable.

Although the cessation of hostilities in the Pacific brought the Avenger's attack role to an abrupt end, the aircraft continued to fly off carrier flightdecks in surveillance and anti-submarine roles until 1954, and even longer in utility roles.

Ironically, after being criticized for its shortcomings, the Helldiver became the US Navy's primary postwar strike aircraft. This proved only temporary, however, with the last Helldiver leaving fleet service in 1949. The SB2C did serve successfully, as did the Avenger, with the air arms of several foreign nations.

FURTHER READING

Astor, Gerald, *Wings of Gold* (Presidio Press, New York, 2004)

Branfill-Cook, Roger, *Torpedo* (Seaforth Publishing, Barnsley, 2014)

Campbell, John, *Naval Weapons of World War Two* (Naval Institute Press, Annapolis, 2002)

Chihaya, Matsataka, *Warships in Profile, Volume 3 – IJN Yamato and Musashi* (Doubleday & Company Inc, Garden City, New York, 1974)

Doyle, David, *SB2C Helldiver in Action* (Squadron/Signal Publications, Carrollton, Texas, 1982)

Doyle, David, *TBF/TBM Avenger in Action* (Squadron/Signal Publications, Carrollton, Texas, 2012)

Eden, Paul (editor), *The Encyclopedia of Aircraft of World War II* (Amber Books, London, 2004)

Field, James A., *The Japanese at Leyte Gulf* (Princeton University Press, Princeton, 1947)

Fletcher, Gregory G., *Intrepid Aviators* (NAL Caliber, New York, 2012)

Friedman, Norman, *Naval Anti-Aircraft Guns and Gunnery* (Naval Institute Press, Annapolis, 2013)

Garzke, William H. and Dulin, Robert O., *Battleships* (Naval Institute Press, Annapolis, 1985)

Mitsura, Yoshida, *Requiem for Battleship Yamato* (Naval Institute Press, Annapolis, 1999)

Morison, Samuel Eliot, *Leyte – Volume XII in the History of United States Naval Operations in World War II* (Little, Brown and Company, Boston, 1975)

Morison, Samuel Eliot, *Victory in the Pacific – Volume XIV in the History of United States Naval Operations in World War II* (Little, Brown and Company, Boston, 1975)

Reynolds, Clark G., *The Fast Carriers* (Naval Institute Press, Annapolis, 1992)

Reynolds, Clark G., *William F. Halsey, Jr – The Great Admirals* (Naval Institute Press, Annapolis, 1997)

Skulski, Janusz, *The Battleship Yamato* (Naval Institute Press, Annapolis, 1988)

Spurr, Russell, *A Glorious Way to Die* (Newmarket Press, New York, 1981)

Stille, Mark, *Imperial Japanese Navy Battleships 1941–45* (Osprey Publishing, Oxford, 2008)

Thomas, Geoff, *US Navy Carrier Aircraft Colours* (Air Research Publications, New Malden, 1989)

Thornton, Tim, *Air Power: The Sinking of IJN Battleship Musashi – Warship XII* (Naval Institute Press, Annapolis, 1991)

Thornton, Tim, *The Sinking of Yamato – Warship 1989* (Naval Institute Press, Annapolis, 1989)

Thornton, Tim, *Yamato: The Achilles' Heel – Warship XI* (Naval Institute Press, Annapolis, 1990)

Tillman, Barrett, *Osprey Combat Aircraft 3 – Helldiver Units of World War 2* (Osprey Publishing, Oxford, 1997)

Tillman, Barrett, *Osprey Combat Aircraft 16 – TBF/TBM Avenger Units of World War 2* (Osprey Publishing, Oxford, 1999)

Tillman, Barrett, *US Navy Fighter Squadrons in World War II* (Specialty Press, North Branch, 1997)

US Naval Technical Mission to Japan, Report S-06-3, *Reports of Damage to Japanese Warships, Article 2* (1946)

Wildenberg, Thomas and Polmar, Norman, *Ship Killers* (Naval Institute Press, Annapolis, 2010)

Yoshimura, Akira, *Build the Musashi* (Kodansha International, Tokyo, 1991)